FOUR CITADELS
&
THE KEY OF TWELVE

CAPRI FAMBRO

AVALINE NINE PUBLISHING LLC

COPYRIGHT © 2021
BOOK COVER BY SARAH ADAMS

PROLOGUE

A newborn child slumbers peacefully afloat in his bassinet amidst a miniature pool surrounded by shimmering blue waters dotted with colorful water lilies. A beautiful mermaid pokes her head above the water to check on the sleeping boy. She whispers, "I must see your grandmother now. I'll only be gone but a moment...sweet precious Nikolai." The boy's nanny slips soundlessly beneath the crystal water where she disappears into a small cavern.

A humming babel, from distant waterfalls, echoes through his bedchamber muffling the sound of heavy footsteps. Chary hands deftly draw in the long beaded tether anchoring the angelic boy to the pearl laden shore. Two roughened hands, ever so carefully, gather up the bundled baby. The child yawns and stretches without ever waking in the arms of the large bearded man with fiery red hair.

"Ugh, Merbatho children — they wreak of weakness," the man thinks to himself. Disgust twists his lip though he gently cradles the small boy...lest he wake. Unwittingly, he absconds with the tiny infant under the cloak of darkness ignorant his deed cannot truly be hidden. A pair of angry emerald eyes silently observe. Filled with ancient wisdom, they ponder the child's foreordained future.

WHEREIN THE LANDSCAPE IS VOID OF TIME
THERE IT BE A FIFTH DIMENSION DOES LIE

A great roar stretches across the Fifth Plane of existence where an argument brews between the four great citadels governing over the four lower planes of existence. The Fifth Plane is comprised of the following citadels: Merbatho Citadel, Aerofin Citadel, Erthen Citadel, and Fyre Citadel. They are pantheons filled with immortal gods and goddesses overseeing billions of galaxies. One, in particular, continually takes up a great deal of their attention—the Milky Way Galaxy—mostly due to one particular planet—Earth.

THE ARGUMENT

The four citadels gather in the Coliseum of Debates with each citadel having one representative on the great floor: Gyntargh The Warrior for the Fyre, Arial The Stormhaven for the Aerofin, Brahmal The Arbitrator for the Erthen, and Surean The Maelstrom for the Merbatho.

The coliseum thunders with the immortals' passionate arguments for and against the humans continued access to elemental majick until finally Brahmal The Arbitrator bellows above all others, "*Quiet!*" The great floor shudders with the walls of the coliseum groaning until all are silent. Brahmal stands tall among his peers, "Enough of this beastly behavior. There will be order in the coliseum or all will be forced to leave, and the representatives will render a verdict in conclave. Choose now." Scowling disgruntled immortals take their seats in silence.

Brahmal motions to Gyntargh, "Please, make your final statement of closing."

Gyntargh rises from his seat and marches stiffly to the middle of the great floor, "It has become too common place for the humans to call upon the *elementals* for their every whim. They have abused the gift we've bestowed upon them. I say each mortal practicing majick must beg from their gods for the privilege of elemental majick, and we will determine if access to the *elementals* is to be granted." Gyntargh strides confidently back to his throne with victory in every step.

Brahmal motions to Arial, "Please, make your statement of closing."

Arial glides to the middle of the great floor, "Yes, it is true that *some* humans have begun using the *elementals* to acquire trivial things. However, many humans remain in humble awe of the gift, using it for that which it was intended; healing, protection, their crops and such. We Aerofin propose sending the mystics to educate those who misuse it." Arial glides back to her throne.

Brahmal motions to Surean, "Please, make your statement of closing."

Surean gracefully saunters towards the middle of the floor. From the corner of her eye she sees Gyntargh scowl as she passes his throne. She can't help but smile, further enraging him. She stands a moment in the middle of the great floor purposely gathering her thoughts. Gyntargh exhales loudly. She smiles patronizingly at Gyntargh before turning to the other immortals. "True, humans indeed use their elemental majick beyond what we intended when the gift was first given, but they've also grown in many ways over the millennia. Given their progress it would be natural their everyday lives consist of wants that are not necessarily needs. However, the gift is still reciprocated with offerings to those of us they specifically call on as well as the *elementals* of whom they ask of help thereby providing balance...and that is, after all, what we strive for them to find. Is it not?"

Gyntargh looks as if he wants to answer Surean's rhetorical question until Brahmal stands glowering between he and Surean. Gyntargh defiantly lifts his chin and grunts. Surean saunters back to her throne to sit and stare unflinchingly at Gyntargh adding a smug smile before turning her head away dismissing him completely.

Brahmal, deep in thought, slowly walks to the middle of the great floor. He stands there silently weighing the words of his peers' individual statements of closing. Raising his eyes to the immortals sitting above him he lifts his arms as if to embrace them all before his deep baritone voice bellows across the coliseum.

"I speak on behalf of the Erthen when I say that we too concede humans have used their gift for purposes not intended. However, the gift was never given with rules or restrictions," Brahmal is interrupted by a murmur rippling through a section of the Fyre members. He knows what he must do.

"I'm afraid this matter of humans and *elementals* has brought us to an uncomfortable impasse with the greatest animosity of division lying between the Fyre and the Merbatho. Therefore, to prevent further division and disruption of the Fifth Plane, I hereby decree the matter to be settled by another *Contest for Conquest* between the Fyre and the Merbatho. Arial, please read the rules of the game...once again." Brahmal grows weary of the ongoing contention between the Fyre and Merbatho Citadels. It seems every 5000 earth years a *Contest for Conquest* is called to settle their disputes over some matter related to humans.

Arial glides to the center of the great floor. Standing with Brahmal she produces a golden scroll, opens it and reads the rules aloud for the umpteenth time. "Each Citadel within the contest will produce one contestant for the *Contest of Conquest*. The first contestant to breach their opponent's portal of entrance between the Earth Plane and the Fifth Plane wins the argument. The losing citadel will give up one of its galaxies to the winning citadel. Safety of all humans is paramount in the game. No human may be harmed during the game. Should any human be harmed as a result of negligence or disregard for the rules by either player then their opponent wins the argument and an appropriate punishment shall be forthcoming. A player may be of any age. The competing Citadels are responsible for the protection of Earth and its universe as well as its humans during the course of the *Contest for Conquest.* Failure to do so will result in the offender or offenders being banished from the Coliseum of Debate for two millennia of Earth's years. These are the non-negotiable rules of the Divine. Let the contest begin." Arial gives Brahmal the look of "here we go again" before gliding back to her throne.

"The argument is closed, and we are adjourned. Return to your respective Citadels," Brahmal's tone of finality sets his peers in motion. He listens to the conversations filtering by him as they file out of the coliseum. He breathes a sigh of relief. The other Citadels, having other pressing agendas, will leave the Fyre and Merbatho to sort out yet another squabble.

Surean, still sitting in her throne waiting for the crowd to dissipate, feels Gyntargh's growing scowl. She recalls winning the previous two contests and can't help but laugh aloud.

Unfortunately, Gyntargh — taking her laughter as an insult — leaps to his feet. "You would mock me here on the great floor!"

Surean, unabashed, looks up still wearing her smug smile, "Oh Gyntargh, you accredit yourself far too much.

Why, I would first have to acknowledge your unremarkable presence before I could ever mock you." Surean feigns regret, "I beg you forgive my distraction. I was merely reminiscing of our last contest...and the one before."

"I look forward to wiping that smile off your face one day soon," Gyntargh turns on his heel and fumes out of the coliseum.

Brahmal exchanges an exasperated look with Arial as Surean's laughter fills the coliseum.

***

Gyntargh storms into the Fyre's Great Banquet Hall muttering under his breath. He makes his way past a throng of goddesses eyeing him disdainfully. Halfway to his favorite long table he hears someone call his name. It's Viktor, the most disliked demigod in the Citadel, best known for his callous nature — more brutish than even the foulest tempered Fyre god or goddesses. Not especially bright, however, he is the one Gyntargh calls on when he can't get his own hands dirty.

"Viktor, my friend. I was unaware you were back on the Fifth plane again."

"Yes, Narceous has me reporting in more frequently these days. Can't fathom why," Viktor grins and tips his mug of dark ale, gulping as it drips down either side off his mouth trickling over a bushy beard.

"Hmph, she still blames you for the ice caps melting," Gyntargh puts up his hand anticipating Viktor's denial, "never mind the song and dance, I couldn't care less. That would be the Merbatho's problem."

Viktor barks out a laugh and puts his arm around Gyntargh. "Great, we can get to business then."

"What business is that?" Gyntargh grumbles before swiping a pint of ale off a pretty server's platter.

"The *Contest for Conquest*, of course."

"What business is it of yours?"

"I know how you can beat the Merbatho this time," he mutters under his breath looking around cautiously.

"Ha, your arrogance never ceases to amaze me. Exactly how do you propose we do that?"

"Shh! You know the rules specify your player can be of any age?" Viktor asks under his breath but above a suspicious whisper.

"Yeah, so what?"

"I've a plan. It will take time to execute—but not to worry. I'm always patience when stalking prey," Viktor grins secretively.

"*My* patience is thinning, make your point or leave me to drink...alone."

"Hear me out. Who knows where the Merbatho portal will appear at all times?"

"*Any* Merbatho knows, you idiot." Gyntargh growls into his mug tired of playing twenty questions.

"Exactly! Any Merbatho of any age! Your player could legally be a young Merbatho. Hear me out now. I'll surveil until I find a young child, one that is susceptible to bribery or blackmail to play for the Fyre. You appoint me as the *Overseer of the Fyre's Player* on Earth."

Gyntargh sets his mug on the table, turns his body to face Viktor, places his hand on Viktor's shoulder and smiles incredulously right before slinging him to the other side of the room. "Idiot, do you expect me to ignore the basic decrees of the Fifth Plane. Bribery and blackmail are forbidden!" Several gods turn to scowl at Viktor wondering what prompted Gyntargh's outburst.

Gyntargh raises his mug to gulp once more when an epiphany strikes. Entranced in his scheme his mug hangs midair as his sits motionless watching Viktor skulking back to his side. *Brilliant, that's what all of the Fyre will call me when we've won.*

A SCHEME'S AFOOT

Viktor slouches down beside him to drown a bruised ego in several pints of ale. Gyntargh clamps his hand down once more and smiles ear to ear, "Old friend, you've given me an idea. There is much to plan," Gyntargh looks around at the crowded dining hall, "Let us retire to my Room of Strategies."

Gyntargh slings his arms around Viktor and loudly requests, "Old friend, you've been gone too long. Come with me and you can regale me with stories of your travels," he leads Viktor through the crowd reminiscing of the old days when the two of them used to travel together wreaking havoc in every galaxy they came upon.

Finally reaching his private chambers, he leads a befuddled Viktor inside motioning he should help himself to the banquet already set to one side upon a long table. Gyntargh seals the door behind them. No other demigod or god will know of his plan. Others in the Fyre will waste time debating their options. Pluto will have circled its sun at least ten times before any consensus is found and Gyntargh is too impatient to best Surean. He fills a platter with food and brings a keg of ale to share with Viktor.

"Tell me Gyntargh," Viktor pauses to guzzle his ale, "what deranged epiphany struck you after having slung me across the Banquet Hall in disgrace?"

"A gloriously eloquent one. I've seen a direct path no immortal has thought of before. It's really quite simple. Albeit it does require your particular lack of virtue and a great patience. In fact, it will take cosmic patience on your part," a secretive chuckle bubbles out ringing its warning throughout the sealed chamber.

Viktor raises an apprehensive eyebrow as he nervously awaits his vengeful friend to unveil this 'path'.

"We're going to borrow a Merbatho infant, take him to Earth where you will raise him until he is capable enough to search and find the Merbatho portal. There will be no need of bribery or blackmail — *you* will earn his trust."

Viktor's mouth drops open, closes, and then opens, "Have you lost your mind? Kidnapping an immortal is forbidden—not to mention me *raising* a child—ME?"

"I said, 'BORROW'. We will return the child to his family once we've breached their portal and won the *Conquest.* And yes, you shall raise him like your life depends on it," Gyntargh leans in closely, "because it does."

"You say, 'HIM,' as if you've already a child in mind."

"Of course, I do. His name is Nikolai of the Mer lineage."

"You're planning on borrowing the grandson of Surean? Surean The Maelstrom Keeper of Atlantis?"

"The one and only. I warned her I'd wipe that smug smile off her face," Gyntargh raises his mug, "Cheers!"

"He is also the son of two immortals I have always given a wide berth—Zale The Cresting Tsunami and Nerida The Sea Nymph—and they are currently ON THE THIRD PLANE!"

"Yes, but nowhere near earth. They're off helping to organize water planets in a new galaxy several light years away. The child will have been returned before they even hear of the matter," Gyntargh offers his mug again with one eyebrow raised.

Viktor reluctantly toasts Gyntargh's plan and wipes his face on his already filthy sleeve. "I require a Guarantee of Pardon if I'm to risk my life for this scheme of yours."

Gyntargh laughs, "Since when do you worry about the rules between gods?"

"Since I'm half human and Surean can end my life with a wave of her hand...and Nerida will most assuredly pluck every limb from my body right before she makes a meal of me for one of her sea creatures."

"Fine," Gyntargh waves his hand and an orange scroll appears, "Here, take this. It guarantees protection of your life and limbs. The blame for any misdeed of our game falls squarely on my head, and my head alone. Happy?"

"Nope, not by a long shot. But it will do."

Gyntargh waves his hand once more and a red scroll appears. He hands it to Viktor, "Here's your instructions, now get going."

Viktor tucks the scrolls inside his shirt and turns to leave. Gyntargh snaps his fingers to break the seal on the door.

"I'll be in touch," Viktor whispers as he opens the door. He shuts the door behind him and hears it seal once more. He stands in the hall staring at the sealed door and grumbles, "Nope, not happy. Not happy at all."

Viktor stomps angrily down the corridor, his steps echoing over the Bloodstone tiles attract the attention of Narceous who is strolling down the adjacent corridor. She stops to listen at the corner. "The sound of a calamitous demigod. Hmm, I wonder," she whispers to herself.

Narceous shifts herself into a salamander and crawls along the top of the corridor trailing Viktor. He stops at the end of the corridor and looks back at the sealed door. "Gyntargh, *old friend,*" he grumbles aloud before heading to his own rooms. Narceous follows him and sneaks around the top of his door as it opens to quickly hide in the shadows of a corner near the ceiling. Viktor slams the door shut, kicks off his boots as he crosses the room and flings himself into a mammoth chair. Pulling out the red scroll he unravels it and reads silently to himself. Narceous quietly scampers along a dark crevice of the ceiling where it meets the wall until she is directly behind Viktor. The scroll appears blank as it is not meant for her eyes. *As I feared,* she thinks to herself, *Gyntargh is going rogue this time.*

Viktor finally speaks aloud, "Hmph, I don't believe I've actually ever seen one up close," he continues reading and then scoffs, "No need to be rude, I'm *always* careful." Viktor rolls up the red scroll in a huff, and places it in a ruby box that will open and close for his hand only… courtesy of another Fyre god for whom he did a solid favor. Viktor looks at his empty table and his belly growls. "No need to rush things on a near semi-empty stomach." He heads for the door with Narceous quickly scampering behind him. The door swings wide allowing her room to dash out the door into the hall where she blends seamlessly with the wall.

Making his way down the hall and around the corner his footsteps grow fainter with each step until they are heard no more. Narceous takes her true form. Standing in the corridor she ponders her options.

Should I call a meeting of the Fyre Council or let Gyntargh's cards fall where they may. Hmm, unfortunately as I currently have no hard evidence against Gyntargh, or Viktor I must first wait for Gyntargh's plan to rear its ugly head.

Narceous sighs aloud then proceeds down the hall, but her moods lifts substantially with the notion that Viktor may finally be banished from the Fifth plane. Her glowing iridescent pearl skin literally shimmers up the tall corridor walls.

***

Having egregiously filled his stomach with the finest food on any plane he makes his way to the Square of Commons as the Light of the Fifth Plane begins to dim. Strolling all too casually along its outer rim he makes his way to the tall stone trough wall that feeds the tiny waterfalls on either side of the serenely beautiful side entrance to the Merbatho Citadel. Ducking around a noisy waterfall he dashes into a dense thicket of carefully trained Salt Cedar. Here Viktor crouches beneath a throng of feathery fronds to watch servants preparing the nightly laundry. He notices a female servant carrying a basket full of colorful cloaks that appear to be made of fish scales. She sets her basket of cleaned cloaks down a few feet from Viktor's position. She walks back to retrieve a second basket. Always the opportunist, he smoothly nabs the first basket. Disappearing beneath the fronds once again, he rummages through it until finally finding one that fits. He tosses the basket skillfully back in its original spot before emerging from the trees. Walking slowly—mimicking others wearing the same robe—he smiles with deep satisfaction as he passes without questioning between two guards. Once inside, he follows the red scroll's map which he has taken great pains to memorize that he might recognize all the "land marks" Gyntargh provided. Finding the nursery is easy enough. Not one Merbatho gives him a second glance.

I knew this would be as easy as taking candy from a baby. Reveling in the ease of access to Merbatho's most valuable treasure—the nursery—the despicable arrogance of the self-centered demigod grows exponentially.

He surveys his surroundings. The entrance to the nursery is merely a wide passageway with a high arch above it. Sweet faint humming sounds stream into the outer hallway. Peeking around the corner of the entrance he sees a dozen more rounded passageways. Engraved above one of them is beautiful mermaid—the crest of the Mer lineage. The lineage of the immortals responsible for the first Mer people to inhabit earth's oceans. He enters this chamber, hugging the darkness of the cavern he waits for the child's nanny to leave and absconds with Surean's infant grandson.

Outside the Citadel, fading light leaves a blanket of darkness. Viktor blindly runs the course of the path Gyntargh has laid out before him. Looking neither into the future, nor into the past where lessons learned could have served him this night, he unknowingly awakens Chaos with her nest full of stinging Strings of Consequence awaiting Divine orders.

I have Gyntargh's protection. I don't know if it will be enough or if it will be honored in any measure. Oh well, it's too late now. I am pretty much committed at this point.

He bounces from the Fifth Plane portal to the vacuole of the Sixth Plane where he chooses one of the zodiac's ports of entry to Earth on the Third Plane.

Uncovering Nikolai's face, he muses aloud, "I hope you're stronger than you look. I've got a feeling we're both in for one long adventure. Hold on tight, cuz here goes nothin'."

Viktor jumps into a port of entry and disappears. In the misty fog produced by the departure, a large gray crab briefly appears before fading into the wafting fog.

THE DIVINE

Deep within the Seventh Plane reside the Divine Three—Fate, Destiny, and Fortune. These three sister goddesses govern above all the lower planes and often to the dismay of those immortals on the Fifth Plane. Here within the center of the Seventh Plane lies the Fortress of Divinity, home to the Divine Three. The goddesses may take any form they choose, each having her own preferences.

Fate most often takes the human form of a tall young woman with smooth olive complexion and emerald eyes set perfectly above high cheekbones. Waves of long cascading chestnut hair hang at her feet. Though she appears young in form her emerald eyes reveal celestial wisdom born long before even the immortals came to be. Fate decides long before the birth of human or their immortal gods what challenges should be met during their lifetime. For immortals, these challenges are meant to help them become stronger, wiser, empathetic to humans, etc...

Her sister Destiny also prefers the human form of a tall woman, but one of slightly more advanced years. She wears her salt and pepper hair in varying lengths depending on her mood and whether she is conversing with humans or immortals. Her skin is as smooth and white as a pearl, sky blue eyes rimmed in a ring of deep blue set above a long regal nose. Destiny, knowing the challenges Fate deals to each human or immortal, does her best to help guide them down the paths they choose. Her favorite human quote being, 'You can lead a horse to water, but you can't make it drink'. She is often frustrated with the nature of both immortals and humans.

Fortune, quite contrary to her sisters, is often a fickle goddess with more than a touch of dark humor. If you sometimes wonder who pulled the rug out from under you...wonder no more. She was probably bored. She takes on many forms whether they be pure energy, animal, elemental, mineral, human, immortal, etc... all dependent on her mood, where her attentions lie, or how the stars align and such. She's a "hands on" kind of Divine Goddess while Fate and Destiny prefer to remain inside their Fortress where they may observe all beings from within their own domain. On occasion they have been known to visit the immortals' Coliseum of Debate. Only on the rarest of events do they set foot within the realm of humans. Fortune, or Lady Luck as she is also known, loves physically flitting between the various planes experiencing all the different energies they have to offer.

Fate and Destiny have carefully monitored the issue broiling amongst the immortals since the first secretive murmurings of rescinding the gift of elemental majick they long ago granted humans. Neither goddess approves of such measures, but they resist intervening for now waiting on emerging paths yet to unfold.

Fate's watchful eye peers angrily upon the immortal's plane scrutinizing Viktor and Gyntargh's most recent scheme. Her annoyance grows with each breath Gyntargh takes. Paths she thought set for the early years of the boy Nikolai now waver, constantly fading in and out, all from Gyntargh's unlawful scheme.

"Soon, I will crush this all too arrogant immortal," Fate promises herself.

"Too often he has let ego rule his head," Destiny sighs in disappointment, "Look away sister before you act prematurely. His judgment must come on the great floor for all to see. You will make an example of him when the time is right," she sighs in resignation, "His record shows he continually refuses to acknowledge the signs I set before him. I fear he is a lost cause."

Lady Luck, not yet aware of the terrible scheme, has been amusing herself in the human realm at a casino with disreputable business practices.

Parading this day as a beautiful young blond dressed in designer clothes, she throws downs money for the roll of the dice, a spin at the slot machines, and last but not least a few hands of black jack. Observing the casino is running higher odds in its favor than the norm—pretty much a full-on scam on the desperate and addicted—Fortune lets her dark side out to play with the crooked casino.

"Now let' see, who will be the lucky one?" Strolling amongst the desperate she happens upon a deep-in-debt widow slipping pennies into a slot machine. She sits down at the neighboring slot machine and smiles as only Lady Luck can, "How's your day?"

"I'm still here so I guess I can't complain," the widow smiles wanly and feeds the greedy monster another coin. Three silly cartoon pictures spin wildly until the first one stops, then a second identical picture stops, then a third stops. The monster lights up like a Christmas tree and loud bells ring and ring and ring. One million dollars flashes across the picture screen and the widow is surrounded by cheering gamblers.

"Congratulations!" Lady Luck hugs the old widow and disappears into the crowd.

Feeling good and reveling in her most recent antics she suddenly feels a strong urge to flit back to the old Fortress.

"Strange, feels like it's time for a reunion with the ol' fam," Fortune muses, "I wonder..." Taking the form of pure energy she burst from the Third Plane, skips past the Fourth, Fifth and Sixth arriving secretively in the middle of Fate and Destiny bantering over the recent turn of events in the immortals' ever boring game. She hovers near the doorway in her energy form hoping to eavesdrop.

"I cannot and will not be lenient! When the time comes, I shall skewer the vermin Viktor—Sister, either leave your energy form and join the conversation or flit yourself back to earth," Fate outs Fortune with the usual admonishing tone of an older sister.

Fortune transforms herself into a beautiful statuesque woman resembling Nefertiti of ancient Egypt. She flashes her sisters a wide smile.

"Hello darlings, what delicious sport have I missed? Did I hear you right? That mongrel demigod, Viktor, has been up to no good as usual? Can I join the game yet...sounds like my cup of tea!" She glides over to plant a kiss on each sister's cheek. "I've missed you both," she pouts, "I wish you'd come with me to Earth. I've had such fun and I'd love to share it with you."

Destiny hugs her mischievous sister, rolling her eyes as she does, "Missed you too. We wish you'd stay with us more often. You know there's an enormity in watching over the lower planes as well as the multitudes of galaxies on the Third not to mention the portals on the Sixth. You could be such a help if you only would."

"Yes, it's true," she giggles, "and it's all too boring. I've only come because I felt your energies pulling me home. Now I know why. I've let the humans enthrall me for far too long (sighs) thus leaving the immortals to their own devices. How greedy with power some have become," she lets go of a cynical chuckle. "They actually believe they solely govern all below them. It seems they've forgotten their place, tsk tsk."

"Patience, dear sister. More time is needed for the paths to form clearly." Destiny puts her arm around the shoulders of Fortune, "The time for your intervention will reveal itself soon enough."

"Hmph, so I'm to wait it out here am I?" She walks to a tall window that is actually a portal to the Fifth Plane. Here the Divine can scroll through all that is on the Fifth Plane...nothing is hidden from them. Not even under the cover of darkness. "What shall I do whilst I'm here?"

"Take a chair and make yourself comfortable," Destiny smiles, guiding her to an out-of-the-way corner with a gilded throne. Fortune's current form is a bit tall for that particular corner. She sighs and morphs into a petite pouting fairy with silver wings. "Fine, where would you like my attention?"

"Here," Fate points at Nikolai swaddled in the arms of Viktor as he descends to the Earth Plane.

Fortune sits up straight squinting her eyes, "Am I hallucinating or has that waste of space actually kidnapped an immortal child?"

Fate's eyes flash with tempered anger, "Your eyes see the truth and yet we will still wait awhile longer. The Merbatho have not yet discovered the missing child."

Destiny watches on with concern, "Did you also notice he chose to enter through the constellation of Cancer and the third house? I can feel a strong shift in the balance of Earth's universe. This deed has given the Fyre a most unfair advantage...and without Divine approval."

Fortune sits upright smiling, "I feel it too. My time for intervention is nearer than I'd hoped.

"Look!" Fate points at the portal where the child's grandmother has come to check on him. "She is pulling the boy's bassinet to shore." A scream travels back through the large window reverberating the Chamber of Portals. Fortune dashes over to stand between her sisters. The crystalline bowl used for scrying now reveals several new paths for Nikolai. The Divine Three stand around the giant bowl watching the paths collide, straighten, fade, then reemerge only to collide and fade again.

"See this ribbon here sisters," Fortune points at a particular path furthest from those that fade, "let me intervene now and the universe will regain a measure of balance. Perhaps some of the other paths will begin to solidify."

"I agree, what do you say Fate?" Destiny's tone urges her sister to act now before a chain of events unleash universal damage.

"I see an upheaval coming among the Citadels over this event. I will join the immortals in their Coliseum of Debate as judge and jury."

Fortune smiles with far off eyes, "Yes, I see where you are going with this..."

"When this ribbon solidifies," she points to a silver one, "meet me on the great floor. You each have a part to play there. Do you see?"

"Yes, I will plant the seed to restore universal balance, and Destiny will bring reason where and when it is needed."

Destiny stares into the crystalline bowl watching new paths emerge as her sisters' intentions are spoken aloud, "Hurry sisters, go now."

FATE'S FURY

Brahmal The Arbitrator stands in the middle of the great floor bellowing his rage at Gyntargh who reclines smugly on his throne confident in his interpretation of the Divine Rules. Surean broils with rage upon her throne, imaging the countless ways to slowly drown Viktor once her grandson is returned.

"You've broken a sacred rule of the Citadels yet here you sit unashamed of your foul grotesque deed impugned upon an *immortal child!* Brahmal bellows until the great floor shakes.

"The borrowed child is unharmed and will be returned when the *Contest for Conquest* has concluded."

Surean, no longer able to control her rage, roars to her feet, "A borrowed child without permission is the same as kidnapped!"

Miniature lightning bolts swirl around Surean as she stalks towards Gyntargh. Rare fear clouds Gyntargh's eyes as he waits for Brahmal to halt the advancing goddess. She is nearly at the midpoint as Brahmal steps aside, willing to let Gyntargh pay with his immortal life, but a Divine voice echoes through the coliseum, "Surean!"

Surean's gathering storm instantly evaporates. Blinded by tears, sorrow carries the goddess back to her own throne where she awaits the Divine. Gyntargh thinks himself saved by Fate. Surely, Fortune smiles upon him.

From thin air, Fate suddenly appears in the middle of the great floor. A hush falls over the room as Fate floats inches above the floor glaring at Gyntargh and the Fyre gods sitting behind him. In the blink of an eye she stands bent over Gyntargh. Fire in her eyes burn through him as he feels himself lifted from his throne. Gyntargh flails his arms in attempt to keep himself upright. Gold sparks emanate from the hem of her gown, swirling about her figure until gone is the statuesque goddess replaced by a terrifying fire whirl.

Her voice leaps from the whirl. Thick with rage, it seers across Gyntargh's face, "YOU are not of the Divine. You do NOT interpret laws of the Divine. You have interfered with an immortal child's preordained path. You are hereby removed as representative of the Fyre Citadel and sentenced to six millennia of hard labor in the mines of Vanodrite on the Third Plane. Furthermore," Fate pauses to watch her prey squirm, "your immortal powers are hereby stripped for the duration of your sentence." Gyntargh's flailing arms abruptly freeze and then he is gone.

Fate steps closer to the stunned Fyre, "Leave now to reconvene in your Great Hall where you will wait for me...indefinitely. Any who leave will join Gyntargh." The Fyre members wordlessly rise, shuffling quietly out of the coliseum as commanded.

Surean rises from her throne and kneels, "Please, Your Divine One, return Nikolai to the Merbatho where he belongs."

"Surean of the Merbatho, rise and stand before us."

Surean rises to stand before Fate. A breeze ruffles the neck of Surean, and she turns to see Destiny standing behind her. "Dear child, though the boy's future has taken a turn against Fate's original design, you need not fear. For I will keep him safe on his journey no matter the path he chooses. He will be returned to you when the contest concludes."

Tears glisten in Surean's eyes, "His kidnapping has torn a chasm through the middle of my heart. His time of absence shall seem an eternity for the Merbatho."

"The Merbatho will be compensated for your interim of sorrow while the contest continues," Fate declares.

A nervous Brahmal rises and bends his knee before the Divine, "May I, your undeserving servant, ask a favor — not for myself or the Citadels — but for the Third Plane?"

"We have already foreseen your concerns dear Brahmal. Not to worry. Fortune favors the Erthen this day," Fate's words reassure him seconds before Lady Luck, still in her fairy form, is at his side whispering in his ear. Brahmal reveals nothing with words or facial expressions. Lady Luck throws him a wink and apparates into thin air.

"Brahmal of the Erthen, your path is clear, let your feet lead the way now," Destiny commands. A speechless Brahmal rises and leaves the coliseum without a word.

Fate turns to the remaining citadels and their members, "The *Contest of Conquest* will continue for a limited number of years. If the contest is still unsettled by the full moon before the boy's eighteenth birthday, we will declare a tie and the matter of debate closed. However, any further infractions or deviance from the Divine Laws will be seen as a direct challenge to our authority. Consequence for such a challenge will be an immortal death from which there will be no return.

Destiny tempers her sister's harsh words, "But should there be a need to have clarification of the Divine

Laws...simply ask. We will always hear you —." Fate cuts her off, "and we are always *watching*. Do not forget."

An all-encompassing bright light strikes terror in the remaining admonished while blanketing a collective calm over the Merbatho, Erthen, and Aerofin. The immense light fades and The Divine have vanished.

Surean stands statuesque in the middle of the great floor. Her tears have gone, replaced by an ethereal comfort from Divine energy as well as specific knowledge imparted by Fortune. Now privy to Brahmal's task, she will keep it to herself for to share the secret is forbidden. Glimpses of possibilities imparted to her leave Surean little to no alternatives. She chooses patience, but now must wrestle with the matter of Nikolai's parents.

Surean makes her way off the great floor towards a side door closest to the path leading to Merbatho Falls. She walks alone but for the four guards and two servants who always accompany her outside of the Merbatho Citadel. She walks along the path that cuts through a field of red clover with borders of flowers native to an earth-like planet too many galaxies away from earth that no human could ever reach it.

Reaching down she runs her fingertips over the tops of the bright flowers bright heads that remind her of earth's sunflowers. In response to her touch they turn their faces up and sing a song only the Merbatho and Aerofin can hear. Surean's party of seven reach Merbatho grounds and she dismisses her guards as she continues to the lake beneath the falls.

Reaching the shoreline, she instructs her servant, "Moreno, I believe I would like to think alone. Please wait with Aquila on the shore for me."

The two servants help her into a small boat and step away as the boat seemingly rows itself out to the middle of the lake. Surean turns her face up to catch the light spray of the falls reaching her.

I call to The Divine Three for guidance. Shall I inform Nikolai's parents of the situation or let them be free of the worry, and tell them when the matter is concluded? As mother to Zale I feel conflicted. I want to protect him from the pain of worry, yet if it were my son, I would be furious if I were not told. I believe Zale would also want to be told. What should I do?

A rustling of ripples roll over the water's surface to gently lap against the little boat. Surean looks down over the edge of the boat and stares into the water's surface. Slowly the face of Destiny appears.

"Surean The Maelstrom your emotions run deeper than any ocean on any planet, but you are also one of our oldest and wisest immortals. Let wisdom guide you now. You are at an important crossroad now. Consider all circumstances and options before making your decision. Yes, the decision is yours alone to make and consequences are far reaching no matter your choice. Ask yourself which ones you—and others—will be able to live with."

Destiny's face fades and then she is gone once again. The boat returns to the shoreline and her servants help her onto the beach.

"Moreno, you will find the elementals who bring reports from Zale and bring them to me at once."

"Yes, My Lady," Moreno leaves the beach with great haste.

"Aquila, I am suddenly more tired than expected. I will have Mauldin deliver me to the Citadel's Lake Entrance. You may make use of the water to find your way back as well. I will meet you in the Banquet Hall."

Aquila simply bows her head, curtsies, and wades into the water where she shape shifts into a seal. On earth her kind are called the Roane. She waits patiently in the water as Surean calls her favorite sea horse.

"Mauldin, come forth now!" Surean's command is answered with a great parting of the water as Mauldin breaches the lake's surface. He swims and lays his head upon the sand providing a walking plank for Surean to reach his wide back.

Surean strokes his turquoise neck watching the light glint off his shimmering scales.

"Mauldin, you are exquisite as ever. I don't believe I have a creation on any other plane that is as beautiful or kind as you are," Surean showers her pet with the energy of pure love. Mauldin purrs—somewhat like a cat—with a deep rumbling coming from his chest.

"Take me home now. I am overdue for a rest," Surean sits in queenly fashion upon his back and watches Aquila jumping small waves as she swims ahead of them.

A light breeze kisses the cheek of the Merbatho goddess reminding her, though she sometimes feels all alone, Destiny is always with her.

RESTORING BALANCE

Brahmal leaves the Coliseum of Debate with a determined focus. He runs to the Erthen Citadel and marches directly to his superior, Agrimony The Supreme Goddess of Erthen.

She sits on her throne of peridot situated at the far end of the Erthen Courtyard where a serpentine path cuts through a garden filled with beautiful fragrant flowers, ornamental plants, and towering trees from the Third Plane. Agrimony wears a crown of tiny yellow roses atop her braided hair. Fate so named her as she knew the goddess would be born of both beauty and thorn. Agrimony's words were capable of charming even the coldest of hearts and equally capable of a malice tough enough to slice through man or god leaving her victim with permanent scars—or worse.

Brahmal, finally reaching the end of path, kneels before Agrimony. "My Lady, I bring news from the Divine."

"I've been expecting you, dear friend. The Divine never arrive or depart without the whole Citadel feeling their presence. What news do you bring?"

Fate has decreed the Merbatho child may be borrowed for the *Contest of Conquest,* the Merbatho shall be compensated—though she did not say how—and Lady Luck has given me the task of restoring the balance to the Third Plane." Agrimony leans forward looking down on Brahmal with keen eyes black as coal.

"Then I must know every detail of her plan, and you will have every asset needed to accomplish your task. But first," with a wave of her hand the two of them appear in her war room before a round table of Hematite, "now we may speak freely. We cannot chance failure by way of loose lips," she motions Brahmal to take a seat as she does. Brahmal sits to her left as his custom. Agrimony pours them both a glass of red wine and hands one to Brahmal. She waits while he takes a long drink and a deep breath, "Now then, speak your mind."

***

As the Erthen make ready for their task at hand the Fyre have assembled in their Great Banquet Hall. Long table after long table is covered with offerings to the Divine. It has now been a day and night since Fate confined the Fyre to their own Citadel in humiliation. In the middle of each table sits a small swirling tower of dense energy surrounded by every delicacy known to be desirable to the Divine. At the far end of the hall the Fyre's Supreme Goddess, Neilina, paces in contemplation unable to anticipate the punishment her Citadel faces. Her subjects line the walls murmuring amongst themselves for it has been more than a thousand lineages since a Citadel was confined by the Divine.

"So, *this* is to be my legacy? It will be *my name* that rains shame upon the future descendants of my line," Neilina bemoans.

She turns on her heel once more to find Fate's emerald eyes boring into her own; measuring her worth. Neilina drops to her knees, head bent staring at the feet of Fate. Fate reaches a graceful hand down to stroke her long thick braid laced with strands of gold and rubies. Much like the humans stroke their favorite pet.

"Rise, Neilina. I bear you no personal responsibility for the actions of Gyntargh. Fear not, my anger has dissipated."

"Thank you, my Goddess. Please know our remorse for Gyntargh's actions and accept our offerings of gratitude for your mercy," Neilina gestures to the rows of overladen long tables.

"Your remorse has been felt and your offerings are accepted."

Destiny and Fortune drop in next to their sister. Fortune takes stock of the offerings and smiles merrily, "I say we have a night of celebration with the Fyre. Let us all feast, drink and be merry as we move forward from the ugliness of the past days."

Destiny claps her hands and music begins to play, "Yes, come now. Let us feast!"

Neilina's subjects flock to the tables in relief, each bringing an offering to each of the Divine and then planting themselves down to feast, drink, and be merry. After the last offering has been delivered the Divine Three they sit back to watch the merriment. Fortune takes her glass of wine and toasts her sisters with a wink before disappearing in a whirl of soft mist. Destiny and Fate exchange a knowing look. One that is not unnoticed by Neilina. The hair beneath her long thick braid stands on end.

Neilina engages conversation with a few of her subjects and begins to move towards one of the exits. She is a mere ten feet away from Door to the Gardens when Destiny appears in front of it. She stands there with a knowing smile. Neilina gives her a small curtsey before inquiring, "My Divine One, shall we walk through the gardens?"

"No, my dear child. It is not a path you shall take this night. You must remain here with your subjects. Continue to honor the one who has shown you mercy lest her anger return."

"Yes, of course. I meant no disrespect."

Destiny leans in and whispers, "True, but I sense deception in an attempt to acquire that which is not yet yours to know." Neilina's face remains as smooth and unmoving as stone. "You are a true champion for your subjects—an admirable quality. Yet, you must accept that you cannot effect any change in what has been written in stone by the Divine. To fight against what has been set in motion this night will only cause you and your Citadel grief and loss. Stand down now, accept what I've told you for it is the best path you can choose."

"Thank you, Destiny, for the clarity. I accept your wisdom." Neilina offers a parting curtsey and returns to engage with the merriment.

BRAHMAL'S PATH BEGINS

The Diving Three return to the Seventh Plane not long after the night of feasting in the Fyre Citadel ends. Inside their fortress, Fate and her sisters relax in their common chamber waiting for paths to solidify.

Fortune lounges lazily on a velvet chaise in the form of white Persian cat. Across the room, Fate rests with her feet perched upon a pulsing cloud of energy while Destiny feeds golden apples to her favorite pet —a giant red flying fox—who literally clings to her.

"I see Surean of the Merbatho sitting alone in her chambers," Fortune yawns, rolling over before continuing, "She has vowed to remain in seclusion until Brahmal has completed his task."

Destiny gazes up towards the chamber's ceiling where Fortune has opened a portal of Surean's room, "She has always proven immense self-control when it matters most." Her fox sniffs at her fingers for another morsel, "No more for you my pet." Destiny rubs his belly with one hand and opens a portal of Neilina with the other.

Fate watches Neilina with amusement, "She is too smart for her own good," she laughs affectionately, "Look at her spinning her wheels. She certainly knows something's afoot. Yes, Neilina feels it in her bones. Tsk, poor thing, I'll shall have to make it up to her."

Fortune rolls her sea green cat eyes, purposely making a hacking puking sound.

"Don't you dare hock up a fur ball on my chaise," warns Destiny.

Fortune stretches, sits up and bathes her face with a giant white paw, pausing to taunt Destiny she mutters quietly, "Fine, I'll save it for your shoes."

Destiny throws a few sparks her way singeing her whiskers.

"That's enough," Fate warns, "the two of you are getting on my nerves.

"Ah, compliments. You make me blushy," Fortune's white fur turns pink.

"Be serious now Fortune," Destiny begs as she opens another portal revealing Brahmal and Agrimony still in her war room, "Look, they're nearly ready to make their move."

"Do you think it fair to keep the Fyre— and your favorite pet— locked up with no warning of what's to come," Fortune goads Fate as she lazily rolls over wide-eyed with playful paws in the air.

"Though it pains me to keep Neilina in the dark, yes. The Merbatho were unprepared for an attack from within the Fifth Plane as such acts are forbidden. Now the Fyre and their future generations will think twice before interpreting laws without our Divine clarification."

"And what of the Aerofin, shall they too play a role in the *Contest for Conquest*?" Fortune asks Destiny with a hint of hope.

"Every path of the contest intersects with the Aerofin. They've no choice."

"Excellent, it's been far too long since I played wi—I mean *helped*—the Aerofin."

Fate stares down her little sister, "The Aerofin are neutral in the contest. You'll not wreak havoc among them. Do I make myself clear?"

Fortune feigns deafness earning herself a gilded cage and shackles. "*Fine*, your tyrannical highness."

"Behave yourself, I've no time to clean up another one of your messes," Fate warns.

"I swear to behave myself in matters of the Aerofin," Fortune purrs half-heartedly.

"I'll be holding you to your oath," Fate punctuates her threat with a steely glare before freeing her troublesome sister.

Destiny who's tuned out her sisters watches the Erthen portal. Brahmal has left Agrimony's war room and is walking through another chamber filled with shape shifters; three female, two males. "Look, Brahmal has started upon the Path of Restoration."

Fortune leaps on the back of the chaise completely engrossed in the unfolding scene.

Fate takes note of the anticipation rolling off her sister, "Patience Little Mischief, your time on this path has not yet come." Fortune audibly plops her fluffy white self down upon the chaise cushions. Her cat whiskers twitching in full pout.

***

Brahmal's team gathers around his Table of Tactics. The huge slab of Malachite comes to light with the touch of Brahmal's hand. A three-dimensional map of the Citadels floats above it. He touches the Fyre Citadel and its floor plan appears, "This is the current layout of the Fyre's entire Citadel and grounds."

A gasp escapes a male shape shifter, "How did you get that?"

"A gift from Lady Luck. While the Fyre feasted with her two sisters she paid Agrimony and I a visit. Here, the nursery lies between the Jade rooms and the Amber rooms. We follow this path and when it turns from tiger's eye to garnet, we will be nearly there. The first entrance will be guarded by a pair of white lions. Once inside there are no other guards on duty, but it will be crawling with informants—salamanders loyal only to Fyre."

A female shape shifter wonders, "Are there no care takers of the children within the nursery?"

"Yes, and we must time our arrival during the children's hours of rest when their care takers leave them to take their own time of rest."

"How do we carry a child out with informants literally crawling everywhere?"

"Frond will shift into a cloak of invisibility," Frond's eyes fill with fear and he looks about to protest, Brahmal holds his hand up, "By order of Lady Luck herself."

"I have never before shifted into a form of invisibility here on the Fifth Plane. I'm not sure how long I can hold the form."

"You and Clay will combine your strengths to hold form until we've exited the Citadel," Brahmal explains confident they will succeed, "and once we're past the white lions you other three will shift and guard our backs. Should the white lions perceive the child's scent, you will shift to form an impenetrable barrier. The lions are not to be harmed per Divine order."

"Understood," replies the three in unison.

"Good, let's make our way to Fyre border where we will wait for our sign from the Divine."

SIGNS

Brahmal and his band gather one at a time in the Square of Commons where all members of all four citadels are free to mingle. Above them in the night sky the three moons of the Fifth Plane grow closer together. Brahmal feels the night slipping away. He anxiously withdraws a round gold pendant from his pocket. A soft glow forms in the center quickly shaping itself into a silver triskele.

"It's time, follow me." Brahmal leads them to a nearby park disappearing behind a tall hedge bearing thorny leaves. "Clay, you will stand in front of us and Frond you will stand behind us. Combine your powers and cloak us all." The shape shifters shimmer a moment, then all six are invisible.

Brahmal issues one last order before entering the Fyre Citadel, "From this point on no one speaks."

The group of six move silently past the white lions and into the diamond tower that is the Fyre Citadel. Following the map in his head Brahmal easily finds the nursery. He listens for any care takers still lingering behind. He hears nothing. Tip toeing through the nursery entrance Brahmal senses an elemental. A single salamander roams over each bed for one final check before disappearing down a separate corridor. Holding their position, Brahmal waits until the elemental's energy has gone before proceeding with his group.

A second sign will point to the child chosen by the Divine. A dozen infants lie fast asleep, each in its own bed of polished stone. Brahmal takes nine steps between the two rows of beds. He looks for the next sign. To his immediate right, a small female child stirs in her bed. Brahmal feels the hum of energies out of balance brought about by Gyntargh. A symbol representing both balance and harmony etches itself on the wall above her bed. This is the second sign. Brahmal holds the triskele over the tiny girl until her faint breathing is silent though her chest rises with each breath. Carefully, he lifts the baby girl and cradles her to his chest. Around her tiny wrist a gold bracelet bears her name, Fianna. With no time to spare he nods to his group and they move as one retracing their steps.

Five paces past the white lions a light breeze betrays their deed. The guards roar in confusion for their eyes seek but cannot find the child they know to be near. The beast are joined by a throng of salamanders who fan out in search parties. Ten paces inside the Fyre border, Clay and Frond lose control of the cloak. The party of six flee with the speed of light. The mighty lions pursue the fleeing party with celestial speed. A mighty roar and the lions make a final great leap at the Fyre gates only to find themselves entangled in a giant spiderweb.

Brahmal, Clay and Frond escape with the child, leaving the other three to buy them time. Brahmal reaches the Erthen's Citadel entrance moments before first light. The morning light slips over the spider web releasing the lions as the shape shifters turn to mist and disappear.

The white lions bound back to their post sending an angry roar through the halls of the Citadel. Neilina is surrounded by chattering salamanders. One of them is actually a gifted immortal— Narceous takes her normal form.

"Neilina, they've taken my Fianna!" Narceous is breathless with rage.

"It is Divine will," Neilina puts her arm around Narceous in defeat, "We must accept it, without exception." Narceous crumbles to the floor and weeps for her lost daughter.

Her daughter still wrapped in Brahmal's arms remains in a deep sleep blissfully too young to know of the drastic turn her life is about to take.

Agrimony waits by the Erthen Fountains for Brahmal. The cascading waters are teaming with elementals and shape shifters anxious to see the Fyre child.

"At last," Agrimony, seeing the arrival of Brahmal with the child, breathes a sigh of relief, "Did everyone return safely?"

"We were nearly caught inside the gate, but all have returned safely."

"How is the child?"

Brahmal carefully presents the infant to her highness. Agrimony uncovers a tiny face to find the typical angelic face of an immortal framed in the typical fiery red hair of the Fyre. Elementals within the pool clamor for a peek. Some having never seen a Fyre child gasp in awe. Fianna is a shining beauty.

"Sahana, come forth now," Agrimony commands without ever looking away.

A small dolphin hovering at the pool's ledge shifts into her female demigod form. She approaches Agrimony offering a small curtsey. "Yes, my lady."

"Take her to the nursery. You will guard her with your life. No harm is to befall this child," Sahana takes Fianna in her ebony arms. Gentle eyes take stock of the little bundle.

"Where shall she sleep, my lady. Unlike the Merbatho, Fyre children cannot swim from birth."

"You will find Destiny has made her a stone bed identical to her own. A private chamber within the nursery has been arranged for her short stay.

"I will settle the child in her room and then make preparations for our trip to earth."

"Uncertain and confusing times lie ahead for both children. Remember to heed Destiny's advice in times of doubt and may Fortune smile upon both children. For these innocents have unknowingly become pawns in this *Contest for Conquest.*" Sahana bows her head before taking her leave.

"Walk with me Brahmal," Agrimony leads him down the adjoining corridor and into a rectangular chamber with rounded corners. Three walls, floor, and ceiling are lined with polished jade. The fourth wall opposite the entrance is lined with gleaming hematite. Agrimony pauses with Brahmal in the middle of the room.

"They probably already know, but I thought we should officially notify the Majix we are nearly ready to send the infant," Agrimony lifts her jeweled hand to the far wall, "Majix, be here now."

The gleaming hematite wall shimmers turning translucent, and three ghostly figures appear as shadows. The shadowy figures materialize and step through the wall to stand before their host.

"Welcome to Erthen, it's been a long time," Agrimony smiles at the three women. The oldest woman leans forward embracing her host.

"Dear Friend, it has been entirely too long, and Brahmal how we've missed your face.

"Rionach, you must come back for a visit once this ugly business has run its course," Brahmal offers with sincerity.

"We could use a lengthy respite," her daughter Niamh steps forward to hug her old friends.

"Count me in," a tiny cloaked figure removes her hood to dazzle both of their hosts. It is Maebh, the beguiling and beautiful daughter of Niamh. The original enchantress of the Third Plane where no mortal man or woman ever resisted her charms.

"Maebh, you are stunning as ever. Please, you all must retire to your rooms," Agrimony waves her hand and a small gnome appears, "take our guests to their rooms. Make sure they have all they need or want."

"Old friend, you spoil us," Rionach laughs.

"Perhaps. Of course, you may not think so kindly of us on the other side of this path we have all been set upon."

"We do not hold you accountable for the actions of a fool," Niamh assures her.

"Then rest yourselves for a bit. We will rejoin you after you have taken your meal," she gives each of the women a hug as they leave with the gnome.

The heavy iron door closes behind the gnome. Agrimony places her finger beneath Brahmal's chin and closes his mouth. He blinks twice and blushes scarlet.

"I could drown in those eyes," Brahmal gasps.

"Apparently. Perhaps I should appoint another liaison for the Majix."

"What?"

"Maebh may be more of a distraction than you can handle."

"Do you really think to find any immortal immune to her beauty and charm?"

"You're probably right. I shall ask Maebh to take on another form. Perhaps one of a squat grotesque ogre with oozing red pustules. Only when in your presence, of course."

"My lady—I beg you not."

"Brahmal you've no sense of humor these days," Agrimony laughs casually then turns quite serious, "Let's check in on the child, Nikolai." She turns to the hematite wall and commands, "Reveal that which I seek."

NANNY ALICEA

The blackness of the hematite shimmers, turns translucent, and then opens a viewing portal of earth. Viktor stands in a small nursery giving instructions to a pretty young woman, "And you must take him swimming every morning before breakfast," the young woman looks startled, "I know what you're thinking, but you shall see he is already a natural."

"I—I don't doubt you sir, but I must insist you are present for at least the first time."

"In that case," Viktor picks up a red eyed Nikolai who had been crying nonstop until the young woman came to the door, "follow me,' Viktor carries Nikolai out to the pool. Resisting the urge to callously toss him in the pool, Viktor gently unwraps the boy then slowly places him on the first step of the baby pool. A giggling Nikolai pats the top of the water splashing with both hands for a moment or two then pushes himself off the step diving head first to the bottom of the pool. The young woman gasps aloud, but before she can leap in after him Nikolai is already surfaced and is floating on his back smiling up at Nanny Alicea.

"I have never—he swims as if her were born in the sea!" Alicea stares open mouthed.

"When can you start?"

"As soon as you like," she murmurs still spell bound.

"Great," he delivers Nikolai from the pool into Alicea's arms," you start now. Follow me, I will show you to your rooms."

"Rooms?"

"Yes, you will have your own mini apartment adjacent to the nursery. You may have one half-day off a week." Viktor's long strides leave Alicea breathless by the time they reach her mini apartment. He opens the door and ushers her in, "Wait here, I'll be right back."

A wide eyed Alicea explores an apartment too spacious and beautiful for a mere nanny. Viktor enters the apartment. Handing her a check he reminds her, "He must have his swim every morning for no less than one half hour. That is your first week's pay in advance, and...," he pulls out a credit card, "this is for anything you need for the house or Nikolai," feigning a somber moment he continues, "I promised my sister he would have only the best for as long I remain on this earth."

Alicea's eyes well up, "His mother passed, I'm so sorry for your loss."

"Thank you," a fake tear rolls down his cheek, "I must leave you now. I've work waiting on me." He turns on his heel and all but runs back to his study.

Shutting the door behind him he raises his hand to seal it for privacy, "All is hidden," he walks to his desk and collapses into a large leather chair only to immediately stand and resume his new habit of pacing, "Gyntargh, *where are you?*"

From another plane Divine eyes check in on Nikolai.

"I had no idea Viktor possessed such acting skills," Destiny glares down upon the demigod.

"Hmph, acting skills...I may puke," Fortune skips about the chamber playing hopscotch mimicking a six-year-old little girl with long ringlets bouncing as she hops. With her last hop she morphs into an ancient long tooth beast long extinct from earth, the Saber Tooth. She roars at the portal, assumes a stalking pose, her feet shuffle, her tail curls side to side as she bares her teeth ready to devour Viktor, "Not yet Little Mischief," warns Fate.

Fortune lets out a huff, morphs into a bat and flies over to hang next to Destiny's flying fox—giving her back to her sisters, "Why must we let him live? He's not exactly irreplaceable." Destiny ignores her sister and continues to monitor the multitude of paths swimming before her eyes. Some of them forming, twisting until they break in two while others simply disappear.

Fate mentally reframes from acknowledging her sister's rhetorical question, because emotionally she would like nothing more than to let Fortune devour the despicable demigod. But restraint is needed. She cannot change the challenges she set in place for Nikolai long before he was born even though they are materializing prematurely. For paths are seldom set in stone and for immortals they do not waver so early in life. Normally they would not be so fragile and ever changing since immortals seldom leave the Fifth Plane where they live by the Divine's strict codes of conduct. Gyntargh's interference has brought chaos to the original paths meant for Nikolai's first few years...much like those of an ordinary human. Fate closes the portal before she loses her own self-control.

Destiny opens the portal for Fianna. The tiny girl lies sleeping peacefully cradled in her bed of polished ruby. Sahana holds a small crystal ball of hematite. The stares intently at it as Agrimony's instructions come to her mind's eye telepathically. She can see the home that has already been secured as living quarters for her and Fianna. They will call this place home for the next several years.

Sahana places the crystal ball in one of many bags she had packed. Destiny can see it contains many outfits fit for the time and place they will reside in the human world.

Two gnomes pick up their bags and follow Sahana with Fianna in her arms down several corridors to the *Chamber of Transport.* A gnome opens the iron door and the two enter the small chamber of mixed stone. Fianna stirs in Sahana's arms hearing the quiet humming of the chamber's energy vortex. The door closes and the two immediately descend landing in Fianna's new nursery.

"Did you feel that?" Fortune asks her sisters, "She has already restored the balance of the Third Plane."

"And not a moment too soon. The planet was nearly ready to shift on its axis," Destiny points to a star map of Earth's universe showing planetary changes in real time, "The planet would have experienced such catastrophic weather changes.

"They would have blamed their gods," Fortune, having taken on the form of the white cat again, muses as she floats on her back circling the ceiling.

"And rightfully so," Fate fumes, still irate at the Fyre and their arrogance setting these events in motion. Immortal children taken from their homes and families, possible planetary catastrophes, wasting the time of the Divine—she's surprised her temper hasn't set her to condemn the whole Citadel. "I wonder...Little Mischief?"

"What?" Fortune asks innocently, wondering which one of her mischievous deeds she's about to be admonished.

"Have you been standing between my torment and the Fyre Citadel?"

"If you mean, have I helped you maintain yourself control lest you annihilate the Fyre Citadel...then yes." Fortune flies down to the floor and assumes a human form, "Only because I love you," she smiles with genuine sincerity.

"Thank you, my Little Mischief never ceases to amaze me," she embraces her sister.

"Come sisters, the Majix are descending to Earth," Destiny urges her sisters' attention back to other matters at hand.

Fortune and Fate join Destiny to watch the chaotic tangled ball of paths for Nikolai and Fianna begin to unravel.

"Finally," Destiny breathes a sigh of relief, "their first few years are settling."

"Yes, still we must keep a close eye. Both of them will have an innate ability to find trouble," Fate looks to their future paths.

"Immortals living amongst the humans is a recipe for mischief," bemoans Destiny shaking her head.

Fortune resuming her cat form curls her whiskers into a devilish smile, "Not to worry. I know every game of mischief." Her form disappears except for one cat eye, "I shall keep them in check." With a departing wink of the eye, she disappears leaving her laughter to echo behind her.

"Right. Now I feel *infinitely better*," Fate mutters sarcastically as she leaves Destiny's chamber.

Destiny smiles to herself as she watches the children's paths cross with those of Fortune.

Actually, I believe she will indeed prove best suited for the task.

BOOKS & BREW

"Well this is cozy," Rionach surveys their new book store.

"Cozy? Sure, if you mean filthy, dank, and dusty," sniffs Maebh."

"How about we check out the upstairs," suggests Niamh.

The trio climbs the steep narrow staircase to survey the living area. Niamh heads to inspect the kitchen area, Rionach wanders room to room taking in each of their window views before returning to the downstairs.

Maebh, in the meantime, has taken note of the number of bathrooms and bedrooms. She meets her mother in the kitchen to report. "Three bedrooms, two baths...," she looks around the kitchen, "and a half decent kitchen," Maebh declares clearly disgruntled.

"Maebh, we've only just arrived," Niamh sighs, "and you're allowed to use majick to make things a bit homier—but you cannot change the floor plan of the bookstore." Niamh pats her on the head before quickly retreating to the downstairs.

Beaming with relief Maebh breaks out her willow wand and gets to work on the upstairs living space. By the time Niamh returns to the first floor Rionach has already spit shined the book store and filled it with rare books, maps, charts, and ancient scrolls.

"It's beautiful, mother. What should we call it? Humans always name their little stores."

"I was thinking something simple. How about *Books and Brew*. We can offer teas, coffees, and pastries. What do you think?

"I think I love it as will all of our—what are they called again?"

"Customers, dear."

"Yes, our customers. Now then, I did a little research on these matters and there are a few things we will need for our business. You know, I think this may actually be fun—at least for the first few years," Niamh excitedly produces their outdoor signage, several of the typical office items, and comfortable furniture for their customers to relax and enjoy their books and brew.

Rionach smiles at her daughter's enthusiasm, glad for the respite they can all enjoy even though she senses it will be short lived. "I think you may be right. Hmm, I think Maebh may have finally finished the upstairs."

"Let's go peek." The two women vanish from the first floor to reappear seconds later in the kitchen.

"Welcome home!" Maebh exclaims, "Let me show you around." Maebh gives her mother and grandmother a tour of their now elegant spacious living quarters that no human could possibly fit inside the little building's true walls.

"Oh darling, it's gorgeous. You've done a wonderful job, such impeccable taste." Niamh compliments her.

"She gets it from her grandmother,' Rionach teases, "How about we go for a stroll through the earthly neighborhood?"

"A splendid idea," Niamh links arms with mother and daughter and in the blink of an eye they're at the front door.

"Allow me," Maebh opens the door, closing it behind the trio, "I'm entirely too curious. I noticed there are no horse and buggies but rather various sized metal boxes on wheels they call 'cars'."

"Wait until you hear some of the new words the young humans use," Niamh warns.

"Thanks to Agrimony, at least we have a current wardrobe. I'm sure the key is to spend our first few weeks observing with our ears open and mouths shut as much as possible," Rionach advises.

Maebh giggles, "ears open mouth shut."

"Mouth shut may prove to be a challenge for you darling," Niamh teases.

"Don't I know it," Maebh's spirits are high, "Let's explore, shall we?" The trio circles the block taking note of the sharp contrast of the desert landscaping against the older structures with pitched roofs and brick exterior compared to the newly constructed flat roof structures with brilliant white stucco exteriors and xeri-scaping that blend with the area's natural desert landscape. The women make their way back to their own street coming down the opposite end of the block from where they started. Lights from the open shops spill out onto the sidewalk nearly reaching the lamp posts lining either side of the street with their own flickering lights casting a warm glow down the entire street.

"It appears our street is a bit older than the rest of the neighbor-hood what with the little shops down stairs and living quarters on the second floor," observes Rionach.

"I prefer the older design; makes sense. Quite efficient if you ask me," Maebh stands on the sidewalk sniffing the air, "Mmm, what is that delicious smell?"

"Our neighbor is apparently a baker. That wonderful aroma is freshly baked pie...apple if I'm not mistaken," her grandmother confirms in between yawns, "In previous trips you were quite stuck on lemon meringue."

"Ah, yes. Now I remember. Do you think it's too late to try a piece of that scrumptious apple pie? The shop looks to still be open."

"It's getting late and your grandmother needs her rest, she is to meet Agrimony in the morning. And I'm anxious to sink into that beautiful bed my wonderful daughter made for me," Niamh steps through the front door smothering a yawn herself.

"But mother. It's too early for me. You know the last time, I had a hard time resting here on the Third Plane."

"Yes, I remember now. Alright, you may explore until midnight, but not in your Majix form. You're not to use your charms on the humans. Understood?"

"Of course. I was already planning on shifting," Maebh transforms herself into a brown-haired woman with a simple kind of beauty, "How is this?"

"Acceptable. You will return home before midnight and no one is to see you use majick. Understood?"

"Yes, mother. Of course, I am not a child anymore."

"Take an umbrella with you, the air smells of rain and humans don't generally walk in the rain without one."

Maebh produces a black umbrella in her hand and a full-length mirror. She stands appraising her fashion choice, new hair style, and bare face, "I think I blend into the human world easily enough. Now...I'm off to find that apple pie."

"Bring two slices home with you. I suspect your grandmother and I will be ready for a midnight snack when you return."

Maebh opens the front door with an eye to a sky full of large dark clouds. She fills her lungs with the air, "Rain is on the horizon and the pie shop calls me. I think this shall be a wonderful night."

Maebh makes her way to the pie shop as her mother and grandmother retire to their rooms.

At midnight the large clock in their living room strikes twelve. Niamh appears from her bedroom to find Maebh sitting at the kitchen counter—completely drenched—with four large *dry* pies.

"Sweet child, why are you dripping wet and yet the pies are dry?"

"Because I first delivered the pies—I brought apple, cherry, peach, and lemon meringue—and then I decided to dance in the rain."

"Like a crazy person?"

"No, like a human child I saw this evening—and I was in the back yard, so I doubt anyone saw me in the dark. It was wonderful. I love the smell of the rain still on me."

"I see." *My daughter is more child than she would ever admit.*

***

Rionach arrives on the Seventh Plane with the taste of cherry pie still on her tongue. She stands quietly weighing the differences between the four pies Maebh brought home as she watches Agrimony sealing her war room against prying eyes and ears. She motions for her friend sit with her at one end of a long ornate table with a small box set upon it. She opens the small box and presents Rionach with an even smaller chest.

"Destiny's gift to the children," Agrimony explains.

Rionach opens the small bronze chest to find a fist size stone. She picks up the stone and looks quizzically up at Agrimony.

"A rock. Destiny is giving the children a rock?"

"One divine stone formed from the Solaris asteroid that passes through all twelve of earth's astrological constellations once every thousand years."

"You'll not be including the Ophiuchus constellation then?"

"No. The immortal children will grow at nearly the same rate as that of the mortal children according to earth's twelve-month journey around its sun."

"I see. Forgive my interruption. Please continue."

"From this stone you will make one key and score it in two. Its purpose to be revealed when the children's paths eventually cross and you make sure each child gets one half of the key."

"And when will that be?"

"When they feel the irresistible pull of the majick card," Agrimony hands Rionach a card resembling a tarot card with a unique key on one side and the same key in two halves on the other side. "You'll know when to make it visible."

Rionach examines the key in its whole form. The stem for holding is quite ornate with scroll work. Two gemstones lie amid the scroll work. One is a blue sapphire "M" and the other a ruby "F". Below the scroll work sit the four elemental signs: earth, air, water, and fire. She flips the card over to exam the two halves of the key. The symbols for earth and air have been split in two. One half has the complete water symbol intended for Nikolai. The other half has the fire symbol intended for Fianna.

"Does she foresee any of the Fyre interfering again?"

"Gyntargh acted on his own. None of his Citadel would dare take up his torch after witnessing his day of judgment."

"I assume you've already informed Sahana of the Divine's plan?"

"Yes, she will be expecting your visit."

"How far are the children from us?"

"Each child is within walking distance, one on either side and just south. A ley line runs east to west between the bookstore and the children. Its energy will be the catalyst for their journey to begin when the time is right."

"When will Brahmal join us? I was surprised he didn't descend with us," asks Rionach.

"That reminds me, when you return send Maebh to me at once," Agrimony commands with a smirk.

Rionach can guess why. Her granddaughter's blinding beauty has often been a distraction. She wonders what form she will be asked to take.

"Before you take your leave my dear," Agrimony smiles playfully as a deck of cards appear between them, "I believe we have time for a few hands."

"I believe we do. Two out of three wins?"

"Jokers are wild," Agrimony swipes up the cards, "My deal."

***

Viktor still paces in front of his desk with the carpet wearing thin as he ponders Gyntargh's absence. "What's keeping him? If the debate over "borrowing" the child was lost someone would surely have reclaimed him by now. If Gyntargh was to be punished I would have been taken too," he looks to the sky and mutters, "You've abandoned me here alone with the little brat, ol*d friend.*"

He is lifted from his state of gloom with the opening of a shimmering portal. A tall distant shadowy figure strolls towards him when quite abruptly it materializes in front of him, "Greetings, old friend!"

CORCOTTA

"Gyntargh!" A startled Viktor jumps back involuntarily. A brief moment of relief in finally seeing Gyntargh disintegrates into anger, "Hello Gyntargh, so honored to be in your magnificent presence once again," he bows mockingly.

Gyntargh bursts out laughing, "Nice to see you haven't lost your arrogant nerve."

"Why did you not at least send word as to the general consensus of the Citadels regarding our "*borrowing*" an immortal child?" Viktor's tone drips with a feigned sense of formality.

Gyntargh lumbers over to a large leather chair to collapse. He groans lifting his feet to recline on a marble coffee table, "*Because*, I was rather preoccupied with fast talking my way out of death with both immortals and the Divine, who by the way initially sent me to the mines." Gyntargh looks around the luxurious study with its plush carpet, expensive furniture, and minibar. "Doesn't appear you've been *suffering* too horribly in my absence."

"No, I've only been slowly going out of my mind waiting on *you!*" He growls through gritted teeth.

Gyntargh leaps to his feet landing squarely in front of his old friend. He towers over Viktor lifting him by his neck with one hand until his feet no longer touch the plush carpet, "You forget your place, demigod. You still exist because I will it. Don't forget, I took the brunt of Fate's ire," Gyntargh's voice rises barely above a whisper.

Terror runs down Viktor's spine setting droplets of sweat across his brow, "Forgive me," Viktor chokes out his plea. Gyntargh drops him in disgrace.

Viktor lies slumped against the mahogany desk, head bent, and holding one hand to his throat. He sees Gyntargh's feet turn and walk to the portal.

"We'll speak no more of this matter. The child's safety is your burden. Any harm comes to the boy and the Divine will make an eternal example of you. In the meantime, as you've found capable care for him, enjoy your surroundings. Have a drink for me."

"You're not staying?" Viktor slowly picks himself up.

"Why would I? Can you not handle one fragile human female?"

"Yes, of course. I only thought we could celebrate your freedom," Viktor offers humbly looking to gain good favor once again.

"Indeed, I do plan to celebrate it—back on the Fifth Plane. Enjoy your time of quiet solitude, Viktor." Gyntargh gifted his old friend a disparaging smirk before disappearing into the portal.

"I've no one to blame except myself. This is what I get for trying to earn favors from immortals. If I were as clever as I thought myself to be, I'd have descended to another universe the moment Narceous cut me loose from her *never-ending* interrogation."

Viktor walks around the massive desk to gather his thoughts settling into the huge ornate chair with its mahogany wood and burgundy leather. He runs his hands over the arms of the chair admiring its quality—for human work that is.

On the far corner of the desk sits an expensive tumbler. He waves his hand over it watching it fill with a dark amber liquid, "Enjoy my time of solitude you say?" He downs the cognac in one gulp. Swiveling his massive chair around to face the large picture window. He glares resentfully at the human city. The big window showcases the setting sun casting its blazing orange over the hot expansive city surrounding the two-story house, "When I've finished my babysitting duties, I do believe I shall start another war on this miserable rock and watch it burn from Jupiter."

Viktor swivels back to the desk, pours himself another glass, humming quietly to himself. For the first time, since his arrival in the house, he takes in the exquisite surroundings he must suffer in his time of solitude. Mahogany shelves filled with leather bound books line three of the four walls. Miniature statuesque bookends break up the near continuous rows of books neatly organized by topic. Only the top shelf is vacant of books. Instead, it displays an array of small statues, swords, and a single working antique gilded clock.

Next to the clock is a statue of a mythical creature. Viktor retrieves it from the shelf for a closer look. It is flawlessly carved from gold topaz. "A golden *corocotta*, hmph. Humans do love their folklore." He sets the statue back on the shelf. He notices the clock's hands indicate the time is now 6:00 pm.

"Hmm, I think I'll investigate the dining hall and set myself a feast. Might as well play the wealthy human."

Viktor leaves the study humming to himself as he wanders the huge house in search of the "dining hall". For a scant moment, the *corocotta's* golden eyes blaze red with the swishing of its tail.

**

Rionach stands, "If I didn't know any better, I'd think you let me win," she raises an eyebrow at her host.

"You know quite well my ego wouldn't permit it," Agrimony teases back.

Rionach stands and gathers up Destiny's gift, "A few protections for the journey back," she places several enchantments about the bronze chest ensuring it will not open for anyone except the Divine and the Majix. Anyone else who tries is ensured a paralyzing dose of mind-numbing pain.

"It's been lovely spending time with you. Perhaps I'll challenge you to another game when things settle down a bit," Agrimony briefly embraces her old friend.

Rionach's aging eyes twinkle back, "I look forward to it...until then," she disappears descending to her family's living quarters where Niamh and Maebh await her in the family room.

"Maebh, darling—Agrimony requires your immediate presence," Rionach sets the bronze chest on a tiny Victorian table where it is immediately cloaked.

"What form has she chosen for me this time?" Maebh wonders aloud with more than a little irritation, "This happens every time we're called to the Third Plane. I refuse to take on the tame bird in a cage scenario again. I'm just saying..." Maebh ascends to the heavens ready to take her complaint up with the Divine if necessary. Her last visit to earth required several weeks of living as a large parrot in a too tiny cage. She was forced to morph into a moth every night to stretch her wings a bit.

"My poor child, her beauty can be a curse more often than not," Niamh feels for her daughter.

"Poor child my fanny," Rionach snorts, "she wields it like a weapon when it suits her."

"Can't argue there. Are you going to explain the chest, or must I wait for Maebh to return?"

"It's a lengthy story and will take all of us to bring its power to fruition. I believe you and I should rest while we wait for the "poor child" to return."

***

Viktor sits noisily stuffing his face at the end of a long dining room table that would easily sit twenty people. The table is filled with fancy meat dishes, pasta, warm breads, delicious sweet fruit from around the globe, and a giant mazer cup filled with mead, "Ah, such suffering I must endure," a fit of chuckles over take the drunk demigod.

Overfilled with mead he does not notice the portal opening, "I see your settling into your new home nice enough," Gyntargh sneers. Taking the seat next to Viktor he plops down filling a platter as he sits, "Be a good lad, pass the mead."

Viktor fills another mazer cup in his usual fashion before setting in front of Gyntargh, "I thought you were celebrating on the Fifth Plane with your immortal friends."

Narceous thought I should be the one to give you the news."

Viktor sobers quickly, "What news?"

"Your to be promoted to the rank of The High Planner," Pulling the Rod of Oaths from thin air Gyntargh pushes back from the table, "Kneel for your oath and repeat after me." Viktor kneels before Gyntargh with his heart racing. Only those who show true ingenuity are awarded such an honor. The Fyre Citadel must have though his plan ingenious, "Repeat after me. I hereby swear to uphold the sacred duties of my office," Gyntargh orders in a most formal manner.

"I hereby swear to uphold the sacred duties of my office," Viktor repeats.

"Your oath is now recorded, and you are hereby eternally bound to it. I now dub thee...(deep chuckle)...high...(giggles)...plan—Ha, Ha, Ha," Gyntargh bends over slapping his knee," I can't believe how fast you fall," Gyntargh continues his fit of laughing except the voice no longer matches the god. The girlish giggles sound foreign to the sight before Viktor's eyes.

"What's going on here?" He demands standing up.

"What's going on...(a swishing golden tails grows behind Gyntargh)...here?" Gyntargh shimmers savagely and the golden *corocotta* emerges with eyes blazing. It lets out a roar only Viktor's ears can perceive. Stalking him around the table as Viktor throws powerful energy balls at it to no effect. Those finding their mark simply evaporate. The *corocotta* shimmers savagely intimidating the demigod once more until he's on his knees with eyes shut tight, fear courses through him. He hears the room grow quiet and still. Slowly his eyes open and find tiny feet bound in leather sandals standing before him—-one taps the floor impatiently. He looks up to find the smuggest face he's ever seen on a celestial woman.

"Viktor, the despicable demigod," Fortune whispers viciously, "your luck has run out."

"Fortune, have mercy on me. I was under orders from Gyntargh!" Victor produces the scroll given to him by Gyntargh, "See for yourself, please!"

"If this is a trick," Fortune bares formidable teeth, "I will banish you to the core of Mars where you will remain in solitude for five thousand rotations of earth around its sun," Fortune swipes the scroll from his hand to read it. Her exasperated expression fills Viktor with relief.

"See, I do not lie. This was not my idea."

"Yes, but you could have reported Gyntargh to Neilina."

"How was I to know the thoughts of a goddess. She could have supported Gyntargh's side and punished me for not following his orders."

"Perhaps," Fortune's angry face turns bright with amusement as she paces the floor, "I think you should know."

"Know what?"

"Know what it is to care for something precious. Something that will keep you awake at nights worrying over its safety. You have buried your human feelings beneath armored plating for far too long. Hence, on this day I bring your human feelings to the surface of your soul where you will wear them for ever more."

"What? Why?!" Viktor whines.

"Because you preferred to save your own skin instead of standing up to Gyntargh for fear of reprisal. As a result, two immortal goddesses will carry the deep pain of their loss even though it be temporary... then again, perhaps I should tear you to shreds and be done with it..."

DESPAIR'S LOT

Narceous calls for her servant, "Bree!" A tall young woman with gold hair reaching her feet appears in her doorway, "Yes, My Lady."

Narceous hands her an envelope with her personal seal, "See this is delivered to Surean The Maelstrom, immediately."

"Yes, my lady." Bree tucks the note in the folds of her gown, "Right away, My Lady."

As always, Bree walks with purpose on her mission. Other servants move aside, knowing whom she serves, as she winds her way through the fortress. Finding her way to the underground tunnels linking the Citadels she makes her way down the brightly lit tunnel to the Merbatho Citadel.

Several guards stand silently at the gate watching her approach. Her station as a Fyre servant becomes apparent by the pendant dangling around her throat. Two guards take a defensive stand.

Bree turns on her charm, "Please, I am only a servant delivering a message," she retrieves the note from her gown to show Narceous' seal, "You must deliver this immediately to Surean The Maelstrom immediately. Failure to do so would bring unfortunate consequences."

The guards immediately recognize the seal. Standing down they resume their former posture. Maddox, a tall guard with bulging muscles extends one very large gloved hand, "I will personally deliver her message."

Bree hands the note to him, "Thank you. Your gesture of goodwill is appreciated," she turns on her heel, once again walking with purpose to resume her post outside Surean's chambers.

The guards watch her figure grow faint down the long tunnel. A befuddled Maddox carefully pockets the note looking to his friend, "gesture of goodwill?"

"More like gesture of self-preservation!" His friends laugh loudly slapping him on the back as he departs to deliver the note.

Maddox finds Surean sitting in her personal gardens with her back to him.

"Excuse the interruption My Lady, but I have message for you—the seal is of Narceous of the Fyre.

Surean simply extends her hand in the air never turning around. Maddox's heavy footsteps reverberate the soft grass as he approaches. Surean slightly turns her head away to hide her tears. But Maddox's keen hearing heard them falling before ever reaching the garden. Respectfully, he places the note in her hand, "My lady." He leaves quietly hoping the note will mend a fence long broken.

Surean turns the note over in her hands a few times wondering if Narceous has written to gloat over her crippling pain. Her love for family, especially Nikolai, is her only true weakness. Frustrated with her inability to fight back—to avenge her family—has cloaked her in sorrow, burying her deep in a pit of despair.

"It's not fair. His family is going to miss all of his first memories. I'll not see him take his first steps, hear his first words, see the light in his eyes...," Surean breaks down in agony. Sobbing torment wreaks havoc on the goddess,

Maddox hears her overwhelming misery at the far end of the long corridor. Surean's pain reverberates through him. Maddox falters in his step to catch his breath wondering why the Divine would let her suffer this way. "My Lady, may the Divine show you favor and ease your pain." He closes his eyes and picture the Three Divine in his mind, "Hear your humble servant, I beg you give Surean reprieve from her grief." Maddox steadies himself resuming his dignified posture before proceeding on his way.

Taking a deep breath Surean mentally prepares herself for the unknown contained behind the orange seal. Slowly she opens the envelope to retrieve the note, "This is unexpected," she says with surprise. Expecting the common Fyre message written on fiery orange parchment she is mystified at the crimson parchment—common only in a Fyre's message of despair.

Quickly she unfolds the handwritten tear-stained message from Narceous.

Good morning Surean,

May the Divine show you kindnesses amidst this time of loss. Please accept my condolences. Your grandson and my daughter have been drug into a game never meant for children. I cannot fathom the Divine's rationale for permitting it. If only I'd known of Gyntargh's scheme I'd have brought him before Neilina for the severe punishment he rightly deserves, and spared our hearts the grief they now drown in. If I hear of any news regarding your Nikolai, I will pass it forward to you, and hope you might return the favor should you hear of my Fianna.
Narceous

"What is this? Her daughter has been taken, too? Surely not by the Merbatho, I did not—would not—request such a deplorable act."

From the Seventh Plane Destiny watches the scene, among many others, unfold before her. She calls mentally to her sister, "There is one upon the Fifth Plane deserving of a change in her luck. Fortune, see her now."

Standing over a cowering demigod, Fortune's fury is in full bloom. Viktor cowers at the feet of a gnashing corocotta, gleaming in gold with ruby eyes, where a beauteous goddess stood but a mere second ago. Then strangely enough the beast vanishes.

In a foul mood she reappears in Surean's garden as a flower. *Destiny finds her deserving of extra considerations, but will I?*

PORTALS & PASSING TIME

Narceous—lost in the raging sea of emotions that seem to constantly wreak havoc with her logic—wordlessly sips a cup of lavender tea in the company of her BFF Surean. The goddesses sit comfortably surrounded by hundreds of fragrant flowers beneath giant oaks draped with hanging moss. Narceous sets her tea down on the giant toadstool between them. Looking around she admires Surean's newest garden, "My dear, you are a true architect when it comes to manifesting a garden."

"That's quite gracious of you Narceous. I think mine's rather simple compared to yours."

"Mmm, perhaps. Yet, I feel simplicity brings a comforting quiet. I find myself spending more time in yours than my own. I do hope I'm not becoming a nuisance."

"Not at all. Besides, I love your company and—what do the humans call it again?"

"I believe 'binge watching' is the term you're looking for."

"Yes, that's right. I love binge watching their birthday parties. It's nice having them only a day apart. Nikolai entered earth with the Sun in Cancer on July 22nd and Fianna entered with the Sun in Leo on July 23rd. Two immortal ambiverts."

"To be born of two extremely polar signs...makes me wonder if it's an echo of their living as immortals on a plane meant for mortals. Ah well, only a couple more earth months before their sixteenth birthday celebrations," Narceous muses.

The two women sit in front of a portal graciously gifted by Fortune before Nikolai's first birthday. True to Fortune's mischief side, it is a double-edged sword granting them privileged access to observe the celebrations but without any participation in either of Nikolai or Fianna's birthday celebrations. Today they've thus far replayed the children's first fourteen birthday celebrations.

With the win of a coin toss the portal now plays Fianna's fifteenth celebration first. She has unwrapped her last birthday present. Reaching into the box she pulls out a new basketball, "Ah, Sahana this is so dope!"

"Considering it's all I've heard about for a month now I figured it would meet your approval."

"Now all I need is a hoop."

"An anonymous friend set one up while you were blowing out your candles." A blur of frenzied teenagers fly out the back door followed by less than enthusiastic parents. Fianna stands underneath the new hoop wondering who the anonymous friend is.

"Well, show us what you've got girlfriend," her friend Mia winks at her, "Everybody back, give her some room now." The group pulls back watching Fianna dribble the ball. Moving it side to side, shifting it around each leg with the speed of a pro, she runs a couple circles with it before leaping up and delivering a slam dunk.

"Um, wow. Sahana, you never told me your niece played," accuses Sharon. She is one of Sahana's neighborhood friends who also happens to be the school's basketball coach.

"This is her first basketball. She's never played," Sahana laughs.

"I've never seen a girl with more natural talent," Sharon thinks aloud.

"Thank you." *You've no idea.*

Narceous' eyes smile warmly even though she's watched this moment at least a hundred times, "I can't wait to see how far she's come with her next birthday.

Surean's eyes twinkle with equal anticipation for her grandson's coming birthday, "I know exactly how you feel. I can't wait to see what new diving skills Nikolai has learned. I wonder how much he's grown. Can we watch his last birthday now?"

Narceous waves a hand over the portal. Nikolai appears standing at the edge of a massive cliff with Viktor beside him. Surean's lip curls slightly at the sight of Viktor.

"You're not having second thoughts, are you?" Viktor's brow wrinkles with concern, "You can always wait until next year."

"No uncle, I'm merely watching for patterns in the waves. I am ready."

Viktor steps back, Nikolai stands tall with his arms at his sides. Inhaling deeply, he raises his arms then leaps gracefully from the ledge diving towards the crashing ocean waves a hundred feet below. Viktor watches him cut through the water confident he will surface in a moment.

Viktor looks to the sky hoping that a certain goddess is listening, "Nikolai is becoming a fine young man and an amazing athlete. There's bravery I never expected to find.

I am doing my best to nurture the boy. Surean, I hope someday you can forgive me."

Down below Nikolai breaks the ocean's surface wearing a smile of triumph. Extending an arm, he waves to Viktor to show him he's okay. Letting the waves carry him to the shore he lands atop a massive boulder. Jumping over to the near nonexistent trail leading back to the top he jogs all the way back up.

Viktor motions behind to Nanny Alicea who's nearly turned blue holding her breath. Exhaling she exits the vehicle to join Viktor at the trailhead.

"You worry for nothing woman," Viktor laughs as he hugs Alicea.

"When it comes to Nikolai, I shall worry till my dying breath. Why does he have to be such a dare devil?"

"Ah, my love. We are too fortunate to have found you. What would I do without you?" Viktor kisses the top of her head.

"Alicea! Did you see me dive?" Nikolai yells as he tops the trailhead.

"I couldn't see you from inside the truck."

"Awe, you've got to have more faith in me."

"I have plenty of faith in you. It's the unpredictable waves, the rocks jutting out from the cliff wall, the swirling water below that looks like a tidal pool to me..."

"Alright, alright...you don't have to watch," Nikolai laughs as he puts one arm around Alicea and the other around Viktor, "I'm starving. Can we find some place to eat?"

"As soon as you shower up and change clothes. We've made reservations at *Bernard's Pasta House* for your birthday."

"Uncle, you spoil me. You know that is my absolute favorite restaurant. Nobody makes ravioli or cheesecake like *Bernard's*. I love you guys," Nikolai laughs hugging them both as they walk to the truck.

"Happy Birthday, Nikolai. We love you too."

The happy trio's laughter fades with the closing of the portal with a flick of Surean's hand. A sigh of mutual exasperation passes between the lips of both goddesses as Surean hands Narceous her tea with one hand while retrieving her own with the other. Surean looks as though another crying session is on the horizon.

Narceous reaches over to hold her friend's hand, "You know, I share your frustration and pain. We have to remember their memories will be restored and the love we've given them will not be forgotten. For now, it is merely hidden deep within their minds. The energy of the Third Plane masks what once was, but it will return when the Divine sees the time is right," Narceous tries to comfort Surean with her words as well as herself.

"Yes, I know, and I am grateful for your company," Surean takes a sip of tea, "This is the first instance in all of my existence that I have become so aware of how slowly time passes on the Third Plane. How do humans tolerate this sense of helplessness, or the complete lack of control?"

"I do not know. I am not even sure how I have not lost my mind. When I discovered Fianna was taken it seemed the walls of the Fyre Citadel were crashing down all around me. But they still stand and I'm still sane," Narceous sighs.

"I wanted to raise a water spout in the middle of the great floor to carry Gyntargh to the bottom of the deepest of oceans where I would anchor him for eternity. But Divine punishment was even more satisfying."

"Of course, there is still the matter of the demigod Viktor."

"Indeed," Surean's voice is quiet and controlled, but her eyes blaze with fury, "He is the one who actually laid hands on an immortal child of the Merbatho and carried him away from his family, his brethren, and out of the Fifth Plane."

"Our world has never seen such a grotesque deed committed on the Fifth Plane," his actions set in motion the chain of events leading to a second immortal child, my Fianna, taken from the Fifth Plane by order of the Divine. All because of the selfish ego of Gyntargh and his idiot cohort."

"I wonder what the Divine have in store for Viktor. Perhaps they will leave his judgment to you and I."

"So, we will continue to patiently wait?" Narceous asks."

"Yes, we wait. Patiently? That's debatable."

"The two solemn goddesses lean back into their high-backed wicker chairs, each wordlessly lapsing into her own inner realm of contemplation. To forgive or to avenge? Always the one puzzle fit to confound both the human and immortal world.

FIANNA

"Fianna! You're going to be late for school!" Sahana calls up to the child she's claimed as her niece while living amongst the humans.

"Doubtful," she skips down the steps wearing a backpack stuffed with books, "I could outrun that old bus with my eyes closed."

"You know I believe you, but don't forget we're working on improving our humility this week, are we not?"

"Yes," an abnormally loud sigh escapes an exasperated face. She wrangles her long red locks with a pony tail holder, "Can we go hiking tomorrow?"

"We'll see."

"Please, it's Saturday, I've already done all my homework, you promised if I could stay out of the principal's office all week we could go to the mountains, and I really want..."

"Fine, yes!" Sahana shuts down the barrage of words gushing from Fianna whom often delights in proving how her gift of gab allows her to verbalize her inner thoughts in rapid succession.

"Yay, one more dull day of school and then," she pauses to turn hand springs to the front door, "FREEDOM!" Fianna bounces out the door with a wave to her aunt.

Fianna hits the sidewalk at full speed, cutting through yards, leaping fences, until finally arriving at Saguaro High School. She skips up the school steps, minutes before her school bus arrives, wearing her smug smile. Flinging open the front door— head held high with confidence—she strides inside wearing her usual smile. Like moths to a flame her classmates immediately flock to her side.

"Hey girl, great game. You were awesome," Fianna's most annoying fake friend and school snob, Charla, pushes her way through the small mob.

Fianna, having indiscriminately soaked up constant admiration for her skills in basketball during her freshman year, unfortunately found herself in the acquisition of numerous fake friends. Charla was the first in line to needlessly flatter Fianna for her talents. Her true friends referred to Charla as a "suck up" ready to kiss Fianna's feet for a chance to be in her inner circle of friends. In reality, she was pitifully envious of Fianna and the lime light she enjoyed every time she brought her team home victorious.

Eventually, Fianna's attachment to fame diminished. Gushing insincere attention now more of an annoyance than anything else. Although, never unkind to her fan club—trusting a scant few—she keeps the rest of her "friends" at arm's length. A growing lack of patience with their trivial superficial nonsense, coupled with their inability to match her physical capabilities, leaves her feeling somewhat isolated

"Thanks, didn't see you at our after party."

"Oh...yeah. I had to leave early," Charla lies.

"Too bad, see you around," Fianna hollers over her shoulder before heading upstairs to her history class. She takes the stairs two at a time dancing through Mrs. Thompson's classroom door.

"Hey Red! Looking pretty quick on the track last week," shouts Mia Jurgen, one of the her few trusted fans.

"Still haven't broken my record though."

"No worries, I got total faith. You'll go to nationals next year!"

"You know it," Fianna high fives Mia.

Sprouting up during her junior high years put her about three inches taller than most girls her age. This did not go unnoticed by the high school's coach for the track team. She was penciled in for the team before ever beginning her first year of high school. Now she was their shining star.

Right from the start, she was a quick study with higher than normal memory retention that would eventually put her on the honor roll with ease.

Now in her sophomore year, Fianna grows restless with the ease of it all. Her "aunt" Sahana feeling Fianna's frustration recently began supplementing her after school hours with additional training in the surrounding cactus covered hills with miles of hiking trails. Long distances combined with desert temperatures gives Fianna the challenge she craves. Hence, Fianna spends every weekend stretching her long legs for miles, winding her way through the saguaro and prickly pear, under the blazing sun.

The first class bell rings loudly. "Okay everyone, take your seats now," Mrs. Thompson shouts over her students. Shuffling papers on her desk, waiting for the class to settle, she walks to the front of her desk to lean on it.

"Good morning, I can see by all your enthusiastic faces that today is indeed Monday."

The class responds with a collective groan. Dylan, the class clown slumping in his chair whines, "Can someone wake me when it's over?" Throwing his head backwards he demonstrates how annoyingly loud he can snore.

Mrs. Thompson offers another option, "I thought we'd all get out of the classroom today. Change things up a bit," Dylan sits up all ears now, "I've made a scavenger hunt." She hands a stack of papers to each student at the front of the class. Waiting patiently until all have been passed to the back of the rows.

"Now then, today we will descend upon our unsuspecting librarian for our scavenger hunt. Each of you will use the online catalogue to find books within our own library to cover each topic listed on your scavenger's list," a collective groan rolls through the room once more, "There are ten topics, each worth ten points. You must find at least two sources for each topic you find today. We will be visiting the library twice more this week. Over the weekend you will use your sources to right out an outline for your report on...*Energy Vortexes of the Southwest*. Now then, everybody line up at the door and we'll get this show on the road."

A curious Fianna anxious to learn something new jumps to be front of the line, "Energy Vortexes? That sounds Uber cool!"

Her fan club, none of whom have any idea of what a vortex might be, scurries to fall in line behind her verbalizing their clueless support for Fianna's enthusiasm. The girl who strong armed her way to stand directly behind Fianna asks, "Energy vortexes? Cool. Is that a drink?"

"No dear, it's not." Mrs. Thompson mentally rolls her eyes as she opens the door to lead the class to the library. *Summer vacation is nearly here. I can make it.* "Alright, no talking in the hallways and stay in line."

***

Fianna spends the rest of her day pouring over her library books while her teachers explain the class lessons on the chalkboard. Of course, Fianna never needs help with her lessons, so her nose being buried in books during class is overlooked. After school she heads straight home feeling famished.

She heads straight for the kitchen where Sahana has left her a snack platter full of high carb foods, "I thought you might want to load up today for your run tomorrow."

Fianna's smile shows off her perfect teeth, "You thought right, as usual." Fianna stacks her library books on the table. Sitting down she stuffs her face with one hand while reading a book with the other.

Sahana picks up the other books, "What's all this?"

Fianna swallows loudly, "New assignment in from Mrs. Thompson. She's given us a scavenger hunt for books covering the topic of *Energy Vortexes of the Southwest.* Why haven't I ever heard of these? Totally cool stuff here," she gulps down her kale shake, "We should take a road trip this summer?"

"To locate vortexes?"

"Yeah, wouldn't it be cool if you can actually feel them?"

"Absolutely, too cool."

Fianna stuffs all her books under one arm, grabs her backpack and another sandwich, "I'm gonna grab a shower, finish reading my books and make some notes tonight. This weekend is already reserved for training," she dashes up the stairs two at a time.

"Alrighty then," Sahana laughs.

***

Fianna stands at the top of the hiking trail with Sahana next to her. Looking down at the hazy city with waves of heat rising up Fianna wonders aloud, "I wonder if there are any bookstores near us. One of my library books mentions something called ley lines. I tried all last night to look them up online, but the WIFI kept freezing up. I tried finding an old fashion printed phone book in the house, but no luck there either. We should get one for back up. But it's all good. Where there's a will there's a way—and as you constantly remind me—I have one strong will." Fianna sprints back down the path with Sahana on her heels.

NIKOLAI

A mile west of Fianna's home Nikolai sits in his uncle's study deep in contemplation. When Viktor realized his immortal nephew was out pacing his human class mates at an early age he opted to give him unrestricted access to his personal library. Nikolai was by nature inexhaustibly curious requiring substantially advanced reading material. His identic memory advanced him far beyond his school teachers leaving them confounded as to why he was not at University already. Viktor used the excuse of emotional immaturity which—in part—was true.

"Nikolai, it's Saturday. Shouldn't you be getting ready to meet Professor Trimble for lunch?"

"I need to cancel today," Nikolai sits with his chin on folded arms staring at the activities within a huge fish tank, "I've a puzzle to work out today. Could you please call him for me?"

Viktor notices an open book for advanced college students, "I suppose that would depend on the puzzle. What are you working on now?" Viktor asks with admiration. Picking up the book he sees its topic covers a theory of multiple dimensions.

Nikolai sighs before sitting up to address his uncle, "Have you ever noticed how the fish swim around their world completely oblivious to the outside world. They know nothing of the vastness beyond the four glass panes literally holding their fragile world together."

"I admit, I've actually never considered the perspective, or the lack of perspective, from the viewpoint of a fish."

"Well I have. I wonder if there is someone—or something—that watches us from other dimensions," a frown creases his brow.

"That is certainly a worthy puzzle. I will make apologies for your absence today," Viktor sets the book back down to leave Nikolai in contemplation. He pauses at the door, "By the way your book, *Geology of the Southwest,* arrived early this morning."

Nikolai already immersed in thoughts of the cosmos with his eyes fixated on the fish tank mutters, "Thank you." Viktor smiles, quietly shutting the door behind him.

Strolling out the back door he stares out over the city recalling the first time he sat in his study viewing the same scene. Only then his cold heart brimmed with malicious intent. Waves of shame and self-loathing wash over him.

"I did not imagine the black heart that I was could ever change. I owe this boy my life. He has grown so strong, swift, and his mind is like a steel trap. How many immortals can boast an identic memory? Not as many as you would think. How many humans, let alone *teenagers,* put down their electronic devices long enough to contemplate the possibility of other dimensions? If only I could undo what I have done, he would be flourishing on the Fifth Plane where he belongs," Viktor chastises himself aloud as it has become his custom.

Footsteps running through the house find their way to the back porch, "Uncle, can we take a road trip this summer? Nikolai stands behind him holding his new book, "There are so many places we need to see. Just look at these cross formations," Nikolai turns the book around to show him the pictures.

"Those are pretty amazing. Why don't you make us a list of all the places you want to see this summer?"

"I've already catalogued the ones in this book. I wish there were a bookstore near us. Ordering online takes too long. I need more resources to make us an adequate itinerary."

"Can't you find your books online?"

"It's not the same. I prefer perusing the shelves of a bookstore where I can inspect them in person."

"Ah, I do understand that," Viktor acknowledges, "How about after lunch we search online to see what our options are?

"Awesome. By the way, I believe I have solved my puzzle."

"I'm eager to hear your solution. Let's go inside, I think I shall need a comfortable chair for this discussion."

"That is probably wise. You're getting older and too much time in the hot sun is not advisable," Nikolai states matter of factly. Viktor heads back inside laughing good heartedly the whole way.

It was well after lunch time when Nikolai finished his theory of the cosmos. Dipping his french fry in ketchup Nikolai looks curiously at Viktor for his response. Shoving another french fry in his mouth he prods Viktor who has been silent longer than Nikolai can bear, "Well, what do you think?"

"I think you have a sound theory. Perhaps next year I should send you to the university. But for now, I think you should get some exercise. Why don't you swim some laps in the pool? Clear your head."

"Yes, I always think better after I work out," Nikolai agrees, already heading to the pool.

Never before had Viktor dared to make a plea to The Divine, but this day he was overcome with guilt and emotion for the boy. He knows Nikolai is too much for this limited world. How could he become all that he was meant to be without the guidance of his family and Citadel?

Filling the long table in the "dining hall" with a variety of delicatessens, he pours a glass of rare wine from an earth vineyard. Kneeling he whispers, "Please. I beg not for myself, but for the innocent—Nikolai. Know my troubled heart. Do not let Nikolai suffer from the consequences put in motion by Gyntargh's treacherous heart. He does not deserve to travel this journey alone bereft of company his own age. My own arrogance was short sighted and selfish. I willingly accept the folly reserved for me, but I beg you to help Nikolai. Here his talents are stifled in this human world. I fear he hides a great sadness from me."

His plea is met with genuine shock, "Didn't see that coming," Fate muses. Destiny smiles knowingly to herself.

Fortune, hiding within a small hollow statue in the far corner, quickly ascends to her sisters. "Well...I guess annihilating Viktor The Despicable is out of the question now," she bemoans.

"He is changed. It appears Nikolai has saved him from himself. "Don't look so disappointed My Little Mischief," Fate scolds.

"I suppose I shouldn't. Destiny? Has his plea affected the time the children's path's will cross?"

"Come and see for yourselves," Destiny is beaming with joy. Her sisters join her at the crystal bowl. An entanglement of obstacles standing between the children fade and disappear. Their independent paths slowly move towards each other now.

"The vibrations of the ley line sitting to their north is no longer muted. See how it calls to them," Destiny points to a thin beam of light crossing the bowl. It's thrumming reaching to either side of the crystal bowl.

"I am relieved to see they won't be alone anymore," Fate sighs with relief, "Their solitude from other immortal children has been a terrible weight for me. I had not perceived its magnitude when I allowed the Contest for Conquest to continue. Hopefully, they will get along as well as Narceous and Surean.

Destiny points to a new path—one that will prove to be an obstacle—it solidifies the closer their paths come together, "They will need celestial guidance. They've come from different molds, Fyre and Merbatho—Fire and Ice."

Fortune grins, "More like oil and water. This should be interesting."

"Indeed. I'm curious how you shall help them overcome it," Fate chuckles watching Fortune's look of disbelief.

FIRE & WATER

Nikolai sits on the grass watching classmates pick their team mates for weekend basketball practice. "Looks like it's going to be boys against the girls again. Too bad," Nikolai sighs in exasperation. He was hoping for a change in their routine. Estimating probabilities for new variables would be much more fun. Now he must find another way to spend his Sunday.

Nikolai stands up brushing dead grass from his cargo pants as he walks towards the street. A basketball comes flying past his head at the same time a member of the boy's team cries out, "My ankle, I rolled it!"

A tall red headed girl runs to the fence as the boy hobbles off the court, "Hey, would you mind tossing me the ball?"

Nikolai picks up the ball, gauges the distance to the basket, and hurls it like a rocket. The rim catches the ball sending it swirling down the net, "Wow, that's pretty good," Fianna compliments him.

"Pff, as if throwing a ball is actually difficult on any level," Nikolai scoffs to himself as he walks off.

"Really, rude much? So, you can shoot a cannon one time, big deal. The question is—can you even play the game?" She laughs sarcastically, "I bet you'd crap out ten minutes into the game," Fianna throws an over-the-shoulder dare as she hurries off.

Nikolai picks up the insulting gauntlet and quickly closes the distance, "Wanna bet?"

"Bet," Fianna turns to face her challenger expecting a boy at least an inch or two shorter. Instead she finds her own green eyes squarely matched by Nikolai's violet eyes mere inches away.

Nikolai smiles inwardly seeing the surprise in Fianna's face. No longer wearing his usual slouch he's much taller than she'd first thought. "Prepare to be humbled," Nikolai warns, but not without sympathy. He's watched her endless victories, always won too easily, many times. Never one to relish in bragging or needing the approval of other children his own age he truly felt sorry for the girl.

"You do realize who I am? I've yet to be *humbled*."

"And I am sorry, your fall shall be infamous. After you," Nikolai flourishes his hand towards the court with a small bow.

Fianna throws him a gruesome glare making her face feel quite strange. Nasty looks not being her norm. She realizes the boy doesn't play for bragging rights, but to meet the challenge she put before him. Most players give their game away after opening their mouths for two minutes. This boy has barely spoken a word compared to most of the hear-my-ego-roar players she's used to. Her empathic nature senses the energy around him. Despite his calm smooth surface there's a fierce undercurrent he hides all too confidently. *What's he hiding?*

"Do you go to school here?" Fianna's own curiosity irritates her, "Not that I care, but I keep a list."

"Yes—when I can bare the tedium of it all," Nikolai confesses, "What do you mean 'a list'?"

"I call it my 'Wall of Defeated'. It holds the name of every school and kid I've ever chewed up and spit out in the name of b-ball or track."

Nikolai bursts out laughing. Not because he was particularly amused, but he rather liked pushing buttons of anyone who dared deny his talented mind or particular skills.

"Why haven't you joined the boy's basketball team? I mean you can obviously find the basket—oh I get it, you've got no stamina. Ha, you probably spend all day with your nose in a book."

"I only play basketball with my uncle. He's actually the only one who's ever made it much of a challenge. And yes, I spend all day with my nose in a book."

"I knew it!" Fianna's smug laugh rings out.

Unfortunately, she is quite ignorant of how Nikolai runs, swims, and lifts weights as much as he reads, "Are you always this over confident?"

"What's your name?" She asks ignoring his jab.

"Nikolai, and yours?"

"Fianna, I'll introduce you to everyone. Hurry up!" Fianna stretches out her long strides. She notices Nikolai surprisingly has no problem matching her step for step. Even her taller classmates would have been jogging to keep up.

Reaching the court in short time they're surrounded by the boy's team all of whom are much shorter than Nikolai. One in particular, Zach, captain of the boy's school basketball team, appears as the first member of his newly forming fan club.

"Wow! Where'd you get that arm! I mean just WOW! Hey, Fianna use my phone and take a pic of all of us with our new friend here," Zach can't wait to tell his coach about the new guy.

"Seriously?"

"Come on, do it for the gram, he's the best gunner I've ever seen! Did you not see that rocket!"

"Fine, but first intros. Everybody, meet Nikolai. He's gonna take Marco's place today."

Exaggerating an obvious "after thought" Fianna asks, "By the way, how do you spell *Nikolai*? I'd hate to misspell it when I add it to my Wall of the Defeated."

Fianna's fan club burst out loud throwing a few jeers of their own. A tall thin girl with freckles and a pony tail yells, "He look like a carrier Fianna—gotta carry the ball *all the way* down the court!" Another tall girl with a braided pony tail laughs loudly adding, "I bet his momma forgot to pack her little boy's *game*."

Fianna, standing tall and smug, quickly points to each player naming each team member on both teams. The girls graciously give Nikolai a nod to acknowledge his presence. Zack and his boys are nearly euphoric with hope. Nikolai would be the savior their school basketball team sorely needed even if he would not be able to join until next school year.

"Okay, intros over. Nikolai stand next to Zack, everybody else crowd in close. Ready, everybody say cheese."

"Cheese," the group shouts in unison with some passing out bunny ears, making goofy faces, or—in Zach's case—spinning the ball on one digit with the other hand on Nikolai's shoulder.

Fianna tosses the phone to Zack, "Okay, if you're done crushing on Nikolai let's play some b-ball."

"Oh yeah, the stars aligned and our boy Nikolai gonna make it rain!" Zach slaps Nikolai on the back, "Let's strategize." The five boys jog back over to their side of the court. Zach whispers, "We're switchin' up our defense today. Nikolai, you're gonna cover Fianna like a sleeve. Watch her close. She's quick as a whip and she can splash that ball 'bout any place on the court she likes. Her ladies always pick her for the jump ball cuz she always clinches the tip off. We gonna flip that today," Zach gives the other boys their man-to-man strategy, and heads to mid court where Marco hobbles on one foot for the jump ball.

"Your newbie ready yet—burnin' day light here," Fianna paces, anxious to annihilate her newest rival. *I almost feel sorry for his impending ruination—almost.*

"Big Red's big mouth gonna get her schooled today," Zach fires back.

"Shut up, already! You fools get over here for the jump, my ride's gonna be here any minute," Marco holds the ball while still hobbling on one foot.

The girls huddle on one side and the boys on the other side, Marco tosses the ball. Fianna and Nikolai mirror each other in the jump, but Nikolai's long fingers reach the ball first much to the roaring approval of his teammates.

"What the—?" Fianna hears one of her fan club mutters in disbelief.

Fianna quickly recovers from her own disbelief charging after Nikolai to no avail. The ball is already air bound for net. The still silence of both teams is palpable. Even the traffic and birds seem to stand still until, "SPLASH!" The boys roar in unison.

Fianna attempts to redeem herself for her fan club with little success. Though she and Nikolai are equally skilled, Nikolai has been studying Fianna's playing style for several weeks now. Predicting her every move, he repeatedly foils her attempts to fake right, occupies her favorite spot in the splash zone, and easily steals the ball leaving her face contorted in frustration. Nikolai, a consummate master of observation, not only brought his game to court but also his exemplary strategic mind.

Fianna's team, never having had to work for a win, struggled to find a strategy. They never guessed Nikolai would let Zach dunk the final basket. Not that he needed the help, but he enjoyed the grimace on Fianna's face each time Zach gave her a grinning wink. The boys celebrated with high fives. The girls lined up speechless to offer up lame finger-tipped high fives as they skulked off. Fianna, faking the high road, gives each boy a solid high five with a smile. She stands her ground at Nikolai.

"Congrats, I totally misjudged you." *Won't make that mistake twice.* "We should do it again sometime."

"That game was *lit!*" Zach gushes wearing a grin nearly as wide as the manikin smile pasted on Fianna's face.

Enjoy it while you can, she fumes on the inside.

"I admit, it was somewhat challenging," Nikolai wears a rare smile as well enjoying Fianna's apparent irritation.

Somewhat? Keep calm, you can get through this.

Turning to Zach he asks, "If you don't mind, I would like to join your game until your friend Marco is recovered."

Naturally.

"Would I mind?" Zach bursts out laughing, "My man, I was prepared to beg. I never had so much fun droppin' dimes up and down the court."

Zach has the biggest boy crush I've ever seen. I'm gonna puke.

"Same time, same place, next week?" Nikolai plays up the enthusiasm although he does genuinely enjoy helping Zach. Fianna's dark mood turns out to be more amusing than he'd ever guessed possible.

Yep, breakfast's getting a roundtrip ticket, Fianna scowls at her internal thoughts. The taste of failure churns in her stomach.

"You got it, catch ya later." Zach and the other teammates filter away waving their goodbyes as they head in separate directions.

Fianna starts off for home giving everyone a polite nod with her departure. Nikolai follows suit trailing behind Fianna.

"Are you following me?" She hollers without stopping.

"I'm going home."

He's relishing my agony. Bet he stalks me all the way home.

"So tell me, how long have you been a mind reader," Fianna decides to save face and fake nice, "Nobody has ever been able to block me the way you did today. I could swear you knew exactly where I'd step, which way I'd fake my next move—," Fianna stops short, "I swear you even knew when an' where I'd shoot my three pointer," her face a mixture of confusion and frustration.

Nikolai ponders a few seconds as to how much truth to divulge. Aware he will soon play her again he errs on the side of subterfuge, "Beginners luck I suppose." They both laugh knowing he lies although Fianna's forced laughter falls short of any sincerity.

What am I gonna tell my team at school tomorrow? No doubt cell towers are leaning full tilt from today's grapevine.

They finally reach the corner of Three Crosses Avenue. To their left lies Nikolai's home and Fianna's to the right. The intersecting street lying straight in front of them dead ends two blocks down. Both having keen eyesight spy it at the same time.

"I've been looking for that," synchronized surprise.

"Why have I never noticed it before?" Fianna wonders aloud.

"I was thinking the same thing. How—strange."

I know where I'll be spending my time tomorrow, synchronized inner thoughts.

"See ya next week," Nikolai saunters off turning west.

"Yeah, see ya," Fianna smiles brightly quickly turning east only to scowl the minute her back is turned.

KEY OF TWELVE

Rionach and Niamh sit at a small round table with a crystal ball perched in the center. They gaze into the ball observing Nikolai and Fianna's reaction to seeing their *Books & Brew* for the first time.

"The time is nearly here," Rionach states matter-of-factly.

"Maebh will be back soon."

"There's no hurry. Not yet," a Divine voice fills the room. Rionach and Maebh turn to see Fortune shining as Lady Luck, "These two have naturally gotten off on the wrong foot even though they secretly wish for a friend equal to their own talent—someone to challenge them—and now that they've found one another their preordained challenges will begin to surface."

"Challenges?" A scowling Maebh scurries through the door, in her shrew form. Fate suppresses a laugh at the gorgeous goddess stuck in a tiny ill-mannered shrew's body.

"Fianna is overly ambitious to say the least. While she has empathy at her core it is muted by her pride and constant need for external approval. She must learn to trust others enough to help them as well as allowing others to help herself. In this way, she and those around her will experience the achievement of new heights in pursuit of their goals. For only then will she know and feel true success—and true friendship."

"And what of the boy," Niamh worries constantly for him.

"Nikolai feelings are oceanic and about as controlled as a hurricane. Though he has great empathy within himself, he is too easily offended over trivial matters. He needs to grow a thicker skin. An overly sensitive ego is counterproductive and serves no one. He must learn to pick and choose more appropriate battles for there are times a warrior's energy is better spent elsewhere."

Lady Luck glides over to the small table to peer into the crystal ball. Fianna, wishing she'd never bet against Nikolai's talents, stuffs her face full of cookies attempting to dull the pain of public humiliation. The fading scene is replaced by Nikolai regaling Nanny Alicea with snapshots of his afternoon. She's overjoyed he's finally found friends his own age.

"Finding the lesson in battles lost is a challenge they must both meet, and that time quickly approaches. Presently, their individual personalities are mostly repellant to one another," Lady Luck sighs acknowledging the obvious.

"One boldly seeking the sunlight. She appears so confident yet harbors a sea of insecurities beneath the surface. The other being overly sensitive seeks the shadows. There he mistakenly appears bereft of any self-confidence, yet it flows abundantly through every vein," Rionach sums up her own observations.

"The conflicting turmoil raging inside them is in part because both immortals entered this plane on the cusp of Cancer and Leo. For as long as they remain on this plane both will be plagued with the challenge of oscillating between those energies of the Moon and the Sun not to mention the other planets as they move through the twelve houses," Niamh opens her book of constellations to silently consider their innate strengths and weaknesses.

"Hmm, where is my ephemeris," she asks herself aloud. Finding it nowhere nearby she holds out her hand where it immediately appears. She flips through several pages before burying her nose in it while simultaneously writing down planetary degrees with her free hand.

"Complicating matters further is the fact that emotional adolescence for so young of immortals is raised to the nth power on this plane. Inevitably, there will be a tendency towards impulsive behaviors," Lady Luck warns. "This we must temper within each child as they move through the contest—sound like fun?"

"We must collectively guide them, nurture their positive aspects, and temper the negative," Niamh's motherly instincts take over. Her own daughter, Maebh, was challenging on a whole other level. Surely, she could manage two immortal children for a short time.

"With regards to the Key of Twelve, you will begin and finish its creation on the next new moon. By then, these two children will be in need of starting with a clean slate. Already, they muddy the water between them," Lady Luck does not look forward to babysitting, "On the new moon cosmic energy will saturate the Key of Twelve bringing out the positive energy in both of them. Nikolai and Fianna must each receive their perspective halves the day after the new moon."

"Are we to seek them out," Maebh grumbles from a counter top.

"No, by then the lure of the ley lines will be too strong for them to resist." Lady Luck assures Maebh.

"And their summer break from school starts in two weeks. I'm sure we will be seeing plenty of them,"

Rionach confirms the date with a calendar floating to one side of the table.

"By the way, off subject a bit here, but where is Brahmal right now?" Maebh inquires hotly.

"He's been called back to the Fifth Plane until the children have both entered the contest," Rionach explains his absence.

"Wonderful news!" Maebh shifts into her normal goddess like features. Standing clothed in the finest designer fashion she picks at a platter of fruit and cheese, "Mmm, I've missed this!"

"Yes, I convinced Destiny—who then instructed Agrimony—that his time here was not yet needed." When no one acknowledges her efforts, a weighted hint is dropped, "You're welcome, *Maebh!*"

"Oh my, yes! Thank you, Lady Luck! I absolutely cringe at the thought of eating another bug."

"You are quite welcome, it was nothing," happy with efforts acknowledge she can now make light of them, "I must be going now. Much to do, as always." The glowing Divine gives Maebh a smile with a wink and disappears.

A Divine voice fills the room again. This time it is Destiny, "My dear friends. Listen carefully and do as I say. You must place these on the Key of Twelve precisely according to your charts."

Two gemstones carved into letters materialize on the table in front of Niamh as follows: A blue lapis in the shape of an "M", and a red ruby in the shape of an "F".

"Show me the Key of Twelve," Rionach commands her book of charts. The large book opens to the page where a sketch of the Key of Twelve is pictured with the twelve constellations that contributed to its creation. Rionach places each stone on their corresponding pictures. The entire sketch glows with the colors of the stones. The stones disappear into the sketch, "They'll be safe there until the key is ready for them," Rionach closes the book. The book shrinks to a few inches then disappears.

"Have you prepared the downstairs for their arrival," Niamh takes the half-eaten fruit platter from Maebh, "I actually made this for myself, dearie."

"Yes, everything is prepared. The books of interest are spelled so no one else will even notice them, nor will either of the little beasts be able to nick one out the door in a backpack. In fact, I've even created a cozy little reading corner for the two of them to swap insults and share a cold shoulder. Happy?"

"Did you remember the honeydew tea?"

"Yes, yes. It's all set out."

"And you've provided all the books on my list?"

"Mother!"

"Yes, darling?"

"You are purposely pushing my buttons!"

"Am I? No, I think not. You've such an active imagination," Niamh takes a slow bite of a large succulent strawberry dipped in chocolate, "Mmm, delicious."

A red-faced Maebh breaks out her wand intent on creating her own feast, "Maebh," Rionach interrupts, "your wand is not to be used for mundane activities such as preparing food for yourself. You've two hands, use them."

Maebh's eyes tear up, "I've been stuck eating bugs and mice for months now, and you didn't even have the courtesy to tell me Brahmal left. I could have been enjoying an assortment of mouthwatering dishes for—how long has he been gone?"

"Only three weeks," Rionach smirks. Maebh's insufferable behavior during Brahmal's stay had not gained her any favors from her grandmother or mother.

"Three weeks!" Maebh shrieks a few octaves higher than her normal speaking tones, "I cannot believe how cruel the two of you..." Rionach snaps her fingers casting a sound barrier around Maebh while she finishes her tirade.

A scarlet faced Maebh falls sobbing into a chair to pout. Looking forlorn at her mother she begs for pity, "Mother, would you please make me a platter." Unfortunately, Niamh isn't feeling charitable this night.

"No, sweetheart. I cannot deprive you of experiencing the human tradition of preparing your own food," Niamh's rejection is met with more sobbing tears, "For pity sake Maebh. It's not like you've got to hunt down an animal and kill it with your own teeth."

"No, but that's what I've been doing ever since Brahmal arrived, and I was forced to live like a shrew—literally!" Maebh screeches at the top of her lungs.

"Well then, a fruit platter should be a piece of cake for you," Niamh's eyes twinkle. She returns to her fruit platter to nibble on mango slices.

Maebh stomps to the kitchen to hunt up her own fruit platter. Rionach waves her hand producing her own platter piled high with desserts.

Niamh flicks her wrist to produce a fine wine with a small platter of cheese, "Can you imagine the fire storm when I tell her she has to do her own laundry—the old-fashioned human way.

HONEYDEW TEA

It was a long school day for Fianna and a less than mundane one for Nikolai. Sunday's friendly practice game quickly coined a new infamous nickname—Flameout Fianna—and was all anyone could talk about. A few of Fianna's fan club ended up in the principal's office for their less than favorable behavior in the hallways leaving a couple boys with bloodied noses.

Children stream out the school doors full of excitement. The afternoon is beautiful with signs of their summer vacation drawing closer every minute. A certain electricity hangs in the air around every school aged child in the city.

Typically, Fianna would be enjoying the electricity all around her, but today she stomps across the school's manicured lawn in an unusually foul mood. The idea of hiding out in the bookstore she spied yesterday was the only thing getting her through a day of endless jeers, taunts, commentary and worst of all—the looks of disappointment from her fan club.

Have I been fooling myself all this time? Maybe I'm no more than your average player. I don't get it. I work nonstop on my game, my strength, my speed...

"Fianna, wait up!" Her internal dialogue is interrupted by the last person on the planet she wants to see or talk to right now.

"Leave me alone, Nikolai."

"No. You need to hear me out," Nikolai falls in step with Fianna who never slows down for him, "I don't understand why you're upset with me. I did warn you."

"Warn me? What are you flapping your gums about now?"

"You deliberately challenged me, and I warned you your fall would be infamous."

"So now you've come to rub salt in my wounds? If we were playing one on one, I'd have wiped the floor up with you!"

"No, not here to rub salt in the wounds. I want to explain how I did it. You need to know, because playing one on one wouldn't have mattered."

"I see. You think I'm an average player and you're not. Nice."

"You're being ridiculous. You are a most exceptional player. Do you not see how inferior your opponents are? Because everyone else has including me."

Fianna slows her pace listening now, "What do you mean?"

"I've watched every ball game you've ever played including those out of town. Think of all those games. Did anyone ever come close to challenging your speed, your coordination, your ability to size up their opponent?"

"No, I guess not."

"I personally wonder why you bothered at all. I gave up playing against other kids years ago. For myself, I need to earn the win. *You* have been my first real challenge besides my uncle."

"Really, cuz it felt more like a train wreck on my side."

"Only because I have watched your every game, your every move, your every strategy..."

"You remember all that?"

"I've an identic mind and I'd appreciate your keeping that between the two of us."

Time for new strategies. I'm going to reinvent myself as a player. Then—rematch. Keep his secret? For now.

"Okay, I'll keep your secret. Although I don't know what the big deal is. Why don't you want anyone to know"?

"Do you like everyone knowing everything about you?"

"Don't really care as long as it's not bad."

Nikolai sighs exasperated, "Well, it's not always been an enjoyable experience for me. By the way, refusing to utilize the talents of your teammates makes you even more predictable. You make the game all about you. Share the ball next time."

"That is the biggest load of bull I've ever heard. You are so full of yourself!"

"Anyway, I tried telling Zach and *everyone* else why your so called "infamous fall" wasn't fully earned. You've never seen me play whereas I have watched you intently for some time."

"Yeah well, a lot of good it did. I've heard nothing but insulting whispering and snide comments all day long!" She pauses in thought, "You do realize it's a bit creepy having a stalker in the bleachers."

"I wasn't stalking you. I was analyzing your games. But then they got boring."

"Boring?"

"Yes, boring."

"Well, excuse me and my lame game!"

Fianna stomps full speed ahead. Exasperated, Nikolai drops back to a casual stroll. *There's positively no reasoning with her.*

"Okay, you win. Your game is lame!" Nikolai shouts.

His insult hits home. Fianna throws her head back in a blood curdling screech. To Nikolai's surprise she wipes angry tears from her cheeks. Too late Nikolai regrets his temper wishing he could take back his hard words.

She gets so completely under my skin. Maddening, she's absolutely maddening.

Fianna skips over Three Crosses Avenue heading for the bookstore. Nikolai can't help but smile when he realizes he's headed for the same place. He anticipates her shock and outrage of having to share the same small enclosed space. He slowly saunters across the street quietly whistling to himself dropping even further back to ensure Fianna does not see him.

She can just deal. I've been waiting a long while for a bookstore within walking distance. If they have what I want, I'll be in an out before she can work herself into a temper tantrum. Not that I'd mind seeing her make a complete fool of herself in public.

Fianna reaching the bookstore slips inside without looking back. Letting her eyes adjust to the dim light she wanders over to the nearest shelf of books. It's filled with romantic novels, "Ewe, gross." She moves onto another row skimming several other bookshelves finding cookbooks, self-help books, children's books—nothing of the vortexes, "Excuse me," she walks to the counter where a lovely woman with kind eyes stands filling a large glass container, "Do you have any books on vortexes? I'd like to buy one if you do."

"We don't have any for sale, but you may find some in our store's in-store reading section."

"The what?"

The friendly woman nods towards a bookshelf behind two chairs cozily tucked away in a corner, "Over there we have a collection of our personal favorites. We let our customers read them here in the store, but they're not for buying or borrowing."

The store's front door opens, and she turns to greet the new customer, "Hello, can I help you find anything in particular?"

"I'm hoping you can," Nikolai can see he's startled Fianna without ever seeing her face. She makes a bee line for the cozy corner hoping to find her book quickly. "I've been looking for a book specific to the geological makeup of our surrounding area."

"You're in luck. My family is particularly fond of studying geodes and such. Unfortunately, we're out of stock. However, you can read those we have in our personal collection—in house—or you can special order them. You'll find them over there."

No way. I suffer being the butt of every joke for the entire school day, then suffer his intolerable presence walking home, and NOW he's screwing up this little oasis I found. It's fine. Perfectly fine. I do not have to acknowledge his miserable presence. He's gonna wished he'd brought a sweater. Fixin' to get chilly in here.

Niamh follows Nikolai to the corner. "I forgot to mention," she addresses the two children forcing Fianna to pull her nose out of a very large book to meet Nikolai's deep violet pools of laughter, "we also offer free honeydew ice tea and cookies. Make yourself at home and let me know if you need anything else."

"Thank you, you've been most helpful," Nikolai's mask of manners barely covers broiling chuckles threatening to explode into waves of barking laughter. His eyes having never left the view of the back of Fianna's head. Privy to every tick, every cringe, and every huff of indignation escaping her body.

"Excuse me," Nikolai crosses the cramped space to browse the far side of the bookcase. His arm brushes the backside of Fianna's arm as he pulls a book off the shelf immediately sending electric chills down her arm.

"No problem," Fianna brushes off the electricity brewing in their little corner. Suddenly hot, a flustered Fianna pours herself a tall glass of honeydew ice tea. Picking up a couple cookies she plants herself in one of two overstuffed chairs.

Nikolai follows Fianna's lead. Pouring himself a tall glass of the spelled ice tea he takes one long deep drink nearly emptying the glass. Refilling the glass with one hand, he scoops up three cookies. Cookies in hand, tea in the other, he settles into the only other chair—exactly six inches from Fianna.

Their partaking of the tea creates a subtle change in the little stores electrical field noticeable only to the mystics.

What a relief. Now we can skirt around some of those immortal teenage temper tantrums. Niamh thinks smiling to herself as she winks at Maebh.

"This tea is excellent," Nikolai takes another long drink. Maebh's spell washes over him leaving an agreeable mood behind.

Fianna wanting to appear lady like had only sipped her tea, but the spelled cookies push her to drink long and deep from the tall glass. A most delightful mood eases over her, gently healing her bruised ego, "Wow, this tea is the GOAT!"

"The what?"

Fianna giggles uncharacteristically, "It means *Greatest of all time*. I know, weird. A cheerleader had to explain it to me. But seriously, this tea is..."

"GOAT, I would have to agree," Nikolai finishes his glass, "but it sounds weird. Are you sure you're using it in the right context?"

"Not at all," Fianna admits, "I'm usually last in line to know."

Nikolai picks up Fianna's book on vortexes noticing the cover is similar to one on his geology books. "What are vortexes?"

"I'm not totally sure. It started with a class assignment and I'm still trying to sift through the literature. I was hoping to find additional literature outside of the school library, and when I noticed this bookstore—I had to check it out." He shows her the similar covers between the two books, "Interesting," Fianna unconsciously leans in closer.

"Decidedly interesting."

"I wonder," quietly, both whisper their inner dialogue aloud.

NEW MOON

Far from earth lies a small, cloaked star called Cenadra situated central to the twelve constellations pivotal to earth's astrological calendar. Shortly before the moon's coming transition relative to earth, the three mystics gather to begin the creation of the Key of Twelve. If Cenadra were not cloaked, earth's astronomers could witness a spectacular show with colorful lightening coming from the small star. The three women shower the *Stone of Constellations* with majickal protection. Lastly, additional spells granted by The Divine are imbued within the stone.

"Now, the stone is ready for molding," Rionach satisfied with their work picks up the stone to ascertain its energy, "Yes, I'm certain of it."

Maebh looks at her delicate feet as wet blue sand slips between her toes, "I've missed Cenadra. I think I shall return when the contest is finally over. Perhaps I can bring Fianna and Nikolai someday. I think they should know the full story. Perhaps the Divine will agree."

"Focus Maebh, we've still a long road ahead. We must return now, complete the molding, set the gems, and score the key before the moon's transition over *Books & Brew* begins," Niamh reminds her daughter.

A bolt of burnt orange bursts from Cenadra signaling the departure of the mystics.

The three women arrive "home" with a quiet landing in their secret room of spells where all is hidden from both humans and gods.

"May I have the honor of molding the key?" Niamh holds the stone in awe feeling the sheer power of its cosmic energy.

Rionach produces a thin platter of gold between the three of them, "You may."

Niamh carefully places the stone on the platter of gold as it hovers motionlessly. Weaving a series of looping circles together with her bejeweled oak wand she brings the stone a few inches above the platter. "Is eochair dhá cheann déag tú!" she commands loudly. Sandy particles fall to the golden platter leaving a beautiful scrolled bronze key .

"It's magnificent," Maebh whispers.

"We are to return the excess to Cenadra," Rionach taps the pile of blue sandy particles sending them home, "*Filleadh abhaile."*

"Now for the gemstones," Maebh gently guides each stone to its new home with her willow wand. Each gemstone's color streams down the key stem twisting round one another creating a breath-taking kaleidoscope before fading away.

"Last but not least, to score the one for the journey of two," Rionach's merlinite wand draws an electric blue line down the middle of the key. The key separates cleanly in two with both halves floating gently down to rest upon the golden platter. The electric blue light dances around each key etching their forms into the gold platter.

"Little beauties you must hide awhile longer," Maebh swishes her wand moving them into the chest that once cradled their origin.

"One last deed this night," Rionach sends the platter to hang in the cozy corner meant for two, "Time for bed. We must rest while we can."

***

The sun sits halfway to noon over a neighborhood park filled with sounds of laughter. Summer rays beating down over Nikolai and Fianna as they wave goodbye to their friends. Speed walking their way to *Books and Brew* after their weekend basketball practice having become the norm since school let out for summer break. They cross the grassy field tired, sweaty, and feeling charged.

"Your team is getting better," Nikolai wipes the sweat from his brow, "My guys were loping double time today."

"I took your advice—"

"Shocking," Nikolai intentionally interrupts. He calculates the seconds to receive the usual look of irritation followed by the expelling of a forced sigh to demonstrate her exaggerated dismay.

"Nikolai! How many times do I have to tell you? Do not interrupt or talk over me. Rude!"

"I apologize. Please continue," a quiet chuckle escapes Nikolai's apology earning him an additional scowl.

"As I was saying, before you so rudely interrupted me, I took your advice." She gives Nikolai an 'I dare you' stare. "The past couple weeks I've been working one-on-one with my team. You were," another mind melding stare, "right. Three of them have some serious skills: Jenna, Angela, and Madison." Fianna shakes her head irritated the obvious had escaped her. "My taking control of all the games last year made them lazy. I was selfishly too focused on the win. Next year will be different. We'll be a stronger team."

"You'll be stronger for helping them too. Plus, it feels pretty good helping someone else. Doesn't it?"

Fianna smiles remembering Angela's first successful three pointer. The look on her face was priceless.

"Go ahead, admit it. We both know it."

"Yeah, it does."

"Welcome to the world beyond Fianna."

"There you go again. Spoiling those brief moments when I stop thinking about cramming my shoe in that smart mouth of yours."

Nikolai opens the door to *Books and Brew,* "Your Highness."

Before she can stomp past him, she hears someone call out, "Flame ON Fianna!"

Nikolai follows her into the book store laughing, "Your fan club staying strong and true."

"Thanks to your idiocy."

"That last game, right before summer break, you threw my team under the bus then backed it up over us. 'Twas epic. I thought your amazing win should be immortalized."

"'Flame On Fianna' was the best you could come up with?"

"What? Everyone loves it."

They reach the cozy corner where Niamh's filing books away.

"Hey Ms. O'Shea. Did your new books come in yet?" Fianna asks hopefully.

"Yes, I've left them on the coffee table for you. Help yourself to some ice tea first. Today's a real scorcher."

Fianna pours two tall glasses of spelled iced honeydew tea while Nikolai loads up a plate of cookies to share. Plopping down in the high back overstuffed chairs a collective sigh escapes them.

"OMG, this place always feels so good," Fianna sips on her ice tea eyeing the new books on the coffee table, "Would you look at that?"

"Look at what?" Nikolai talks over a mouthful of cookie.

Fianna put the books next to each other. Their covers similar enough to be two pieces of a puzzle.

"Hang on," Nikolai dashes over to the bookshelf pulling out two other books. He sets them down next to the other two, "Look at that."

"Two books on vortexes and one book on ley lines. All sharing very similar covers."

"They're all self-published by F.D. Fortune. Maybe he/she lacks the creativity for marketing."

"Or...this author is exceptionally creative. What if each book is an individual piece of a puzzle?" Nikolai's calculating mind theorizes.

"That's reaching but go ahead. Theorize away."

"All you have to do is consider all we've learned the past eight weeks and *how* each book led to the next."

"Go on," Fianna slowly chews her cookie. Sensing another of Nikolai's overly detailed theories she sinks further into her chair. *I'm going to need more cookies for this.*

"First, we find ley lines oddly mentioned in one of the geology books discussing different types of sand. That book has an anonymous author. A bit strange for a geology book. Second, there were four references for that book three of which are lying right here before us," Nikolai's long mental list is cut abruptly short, "I can feel the connection in my bones. Ugh, I'm probably never going to sleep again until I solve it."

"Nothing like a good mystery to keep me awake," Fianna agrees, "My birthday is coming up this weekend. Want to come over and I'll show you my map of vortexes. We could brain storm your theory."

"You have a map? Oh, which day is your birthday?"

"Yeah, I've been mapping out my notes on vortexes, and my birthday is July 22nd, this Saturday."

"Huh, my birthday is July 23rd, and I've mapped out ley lines. We should compare maps.

"Did I hear someone say they have a birthday this weekend?" Niamh approaches with two small, gift-wrapped boxes, "Happy Birthday! We hope you have a wonderful weekend."

"Ms. O'Shea, wow. You're too much," Fianna jumps up to give her a polite but warm hug, "Thank you!"

"Yes, thank you, Ms. O'Shea. You really didn't have to —," Nikolai feeling obligated by rules of reciprocity tries to bow out of the gift gracefully, but Fianna's mind meld forbids it, "thank you. It's very kind of you."

Niamh laughs warmly, "It's just a little something I picked up. Needs a new home, this place is bursting at the seams." She quietly makes her way back upstairs before the unwrapping of presents.

SYNCHRONICITY

From her peripheral, Fianna watches Niamh sneaking back upstairs. She waits to hear the upstairs door shut, "What is your problem?"

"I'm sorry?"

"Sorry? Yeah, you should be. Ms. O'Shea ordered books for us at no cost so we could continue our research. Then—out of the blue— she brings us a birthday gift and you were about to refuse it. Don't deny it. I know that 'I don't wanna be obligated' face when I see it."

"I never know what is expected of me when strangers give me presents. I thought—I mean—I was only going to convey that I wasn't expecting one from her," Nikolai struggles to communicate his feelings. Fianna's explanations were always so short and succinct. She made him feel like a babbling idiot every time he attempted a truncated version of his thoughts or feelings which were always too many and far too deep. "I'm sorry. I'm grateful for her kindness. Do you think it would be okay if I brought her a thank you card?"

"Nikolai," her exasperation fizzles out, "being kind really isn't that complicated. Let's open our presents, and when we see her again simply tell her how much we like them, or maybe how useful they will be. Be genuine in a kind way. You make things so overly formal sometimes, you know that?"

"In my family, things are *always* formal. My uncle's favorite saying is how he prefers to 'run a tight ship' and he does."

"Well, he's not here now. Open your present, I want to see what you got." Nikolai removes the dark blue ribbon from the tiny silver box. He lifts the lid. Fianna hears an audible gasp escape his lips for the first time ever.

"Amazing. Simply amazing," he lifts up one half of the Key of Twelve feeling the pull of its energy. Attached to the small key is a silver chain. Still holding the key in one hand he instinctively slips the chain around his neck with the other.

"Wow. I can't even...," Fianna is at a loss for words. Though the key does not call her the same way as it is not meant for her, its beauty is undeniable.

"Open yours," Nikolai's urges Fianna. His eyes still wandering over the fine details of his own key.

Fianna removes the red ribbon cradling her own box. With trembling fingers, she removes its gold lid. She stares momentarily stunned sitting silently frozen until finally sucking in a breath she finds her motor skills once more. Lifting her own breathtaking bejeweled key, she holds it up for Nikolai to see.

"You have one too, but with a gold chain."

Fianna unconsciously slips the chain around her neck while lifting the key up next to Nikolai's, "Look, they're mirror images."

The two keys, held closely together, draw in energy from their likeness that hangs on the wall directly behind them. The gold platter feels their call glinting in the sunshine that seemingly came from nowhere.

"No way. Do you see that?" Fianna and Nikolai stare in shock at the shining gold disc with glistening versions of their keys etched in the center of its inner circle.

"Has that always been hanging there?" A befuddled Nikolai looks at Fianna.

"I don't know. I always have tunnel vision when I'm in here. If something doesn't say 'vortex' on it, I don't really pay it much mind."

"Does yours feel like you'll never be able to take it off?"

"Yeah. The energy coming off it is—,"

"GOAT?"

"No, that doesn't even come close. I hereby retract my former opinion. We are definitely getting Ms. O'Shea a thank you card!"

Nikolai's brow crinkles with worry, "They're quite unique."

"Don't you dare think about giving it back, you'll hurt her feelings."

"I couldn't even if I wanted to, but I also don't want someone mugging me for it so—," Nikolai hides his key beneath his shirt.

"Good idea," Fianna follows suit, "I've only got another couple of hours before I have to be home," she picks up one of the new books, "Research time."

"Right," he picks up the other book and shoves a cookie in his mouth.

An hour and a half later the pair stand on the cross street at Three Crosses Avenue discussing the combining of their birthday parties. Not an amenable undertaking as Nikolai only ever invited other children once to his party. The disaster was memorable.

"Nikolai, I'm not hearing any more excuses. We have more than our birthdays to celebrate. There's an adventure coming our way, can't you feel it."

"Yes, I do. I've a feeling it's beyond our control. Kind of unsettling."

"Synchronicity, that's what it is."

"Now I know how the pawn on my chessboard feels."

"Do you think Ms. O'Shea is part of it?"

"*Obviously*."

"No, it's not—don't be a snob. Do you think she's a willing or unwilling party?"

"Undecided—for now."

"Nikolai!" Charla's high-pitched voice calls out from a group of bikini clad girls leaving the park's swimming pool.

Fianna groans inwardly but smiles and waves. Nikolai smiles awkwardly acknowledging her with a nod of his head. He turns his head away from Charla to mouth, 'Help me' at Fianna.

Always anxious to collect summer gossip, Charla's group encircles the two seemingly love birds who appear to be having a spat.

"Hey, what you two sweethearts up to?"

"Still just friends Charla," Fianna quashes one potential tidbit.

"In that case, Nikolai don't be a stranger. Come swim with us sometime," Charla turns on the charm.

"Sorry, I don't swim," he lies convincingly.

"Too bad," Charla pulls out her lip faking a pout, "Still, I'm sure we can find something to do," a flirty suggestive smile has Nikolai blushing crimson. "Gotta run now, but you should tap my digits sometime, Fianna's got them." Charla departs with a flirty wink.

Fianna's wrestles back the urge to cue ball Charla. She savors an image of Charla pinned on the grass, her hands deftly shearing Charla's head, watching those long golden locks pile up... Satisfaction ever so slowly curls up the corners of her mouth.

"Dodging that one is getting harder. Need to avoid the park for a while." Terrified, Nikolai stares at the departing mob of girls.

"No. Next time I'll stake a claim on you. Then she'll keep her distance."

"That would be GOAT, thanks."

"And to pay me back you'll bring your family to my party."

"I'll try," Nikolai groans loudly, "But no promises they'll come."

"Oh, they'll come. I've got a secret weapon."

"Really? Do tell," Nikolai laughs mockingly.

"One word."

"And that would be?"

"Sahana—my aunt could charm the diamonds off a rattler."

"Bet you twenty." *Your aunt has never met my uncle!*

Fianna heel turns for home with an over the shoulder smile, "You're on," already feeling the win she accepts the bet and ups the ante with conditions, "Don't be late and make sure it's a *crisp* Jackson."

Nikolai happily takes the taunt watching her long stride stroll lazily down the street with dark auburn curls flowing down to her waist.

Huh, when did she start curling her hair? Nice. "Don't be wearing that laurel crown just yet, sweetheart!"

An echo of tinkling laughter dances over the hot summer breeze to chase after Nikolai.

OLD FLAME

Neilina, lost in thought, sits upon her throne staring into a large goblet of dark ale replaying the morning's conversation with Narceous.

"Are we any closer to the close of the *Contest for Conquest*?" Narceous is hopeful.

"Destiny tells me the children's paths have finally crossed." Neilina states matter-of-factly.

"And this is a good thing?"

"I can't say that it is a good thing, but it is progress."

"Does the Divine not give you any meaningful insights?"

Neilina laughs at the notion, "Narceous, you were gifted a portal to view your child's *birthdays* on earth. I'm given cryptic messages a few times an earth year and nothing more. I'm as much in the dark as you are. We are all punished for Gyntargh's callous deed."

"I am beginning to think the mines were not severe enough punishment for my own satisfaction."

"Shh, do not say—no, do not even think of questioning Fate's judgment. Be grateful it was only Gyntargh sent to the mines."

"Yes, you're right. It is not my place to question the Divine's judgment. Fortune eventually smiled upon Surean and I. We are ever grateful; we would not seek to cause any further arguments." Narceous remains mindful of the ever watching Divine Three.

"Mmm, speaking of further arguments, we may have a problem with Idalia."

"Idalia? She has often been Viktor's partner in mayhem, but with him gone I've had no reports of mischief about her."

"Exactly. Not a toe out of line."

"She's plotting, isn't she?"

"For some time now, I think."

"We cannot let her jeopardize the peace. We cannot let her interfere with the contest. Fate may punish our entire Citadel as an example to the others," Narceous' hands tremble with the notion, "Perhaps she should be confined until the contest concludes."

"I am considering it, but without proof of treachery it could bring considerable backlash from the other members of the Fyre. A great division amongst ourselves is the last thing we need right now."

"Then I will have her followed. At the first sign of treachery she will be brought before you for judgment."

***

Idalia sits alone in a far corner of the banquet hall watching the many couples sitting together. There are actually a few members of the Fyre who prefer to sit alone contemplating in solitude. She is not one of them. Her introspective analysis of her relationship with Viktor grows with increasing irritation while she awaits the arrival of an epiphany. Her feverish mind searching for justification of the seed of suspicion growing by the hour has not rested since Viktor's departure with the boy.

Viktor's absence from the Fyre has—surprisingly—brought me an immeasurable amount of heartache that seemingly will never end. Neilina gives me no hope as to if and when he might return all the while keeping me bound here to the Fifth Plane. She refuses to let me search for him myself leaving me to my own excruciating solitude.

I admit my pain is borne not from mere boredom, but true loneliness. Here I sit amongst a crowd of my own brethren. They're oblivious to my pain—to the misery I am cloaked within. Never have I seen myself becoming bound to another let alone Viktor. Yet here I sit pining over an idiot demigod who's yet to show me any loyalty. How could he exclude me from his journey so easily? Still—he is all I think about. He is all I want.

"Well look who's decided to join us for banquet today!" Janice announces too loudly from a nearby feasting table—brimming with curious eyes—bringing Idalia's quiet presence to the forefront of everyone present. An audible hush falls briefly over the hall as all eyes turn to the far dimly lit corner.

"Actually, I'm here quite often Janice if you ever bothered to notice anything beyond your own face," Idalia's cheeks color with irritation and embarrassment.

"You're right of course. It must be your radiant personality that outshines my own handsome face this morning. So good to have you," Janice, rising up from his seat to join her, laughs unabashed.

"What *are* you doing?" Her eyes widen with a slight screech in her voice. Walls from her personal quarters closing in on her had driven her to the banquet hall to keep from suffocating. She did not want or need company —much less from the preening Janice.

"I've come to join in your commiseration. No, don't deny it. We all feel the frustration of our quarantine. For you it must be ten times worse. I mean with your Viktor detained on Earth and your forced confinement here," Janice looks around them, leans in and lowers his voice to whisper, "No one would blame you if you went rogue."

Idalia's eyes spark with intrigue, "You're trying to bait me, aren't you?"

"Not at all. There are several of our brethren filled with empathy for your situation," Janice lies too convincingly. Idalia is as unlikeable as Viktor's old self.

"Thank you, but it's not necessary. I'm coping and will continue to do so," Idalia's eyes confess her lies.

"Well, if there's anything you *need* let me know. I'm at your service." Janice returns to his own table. His group of friends give momentary pause in their conversation to read his face dripping with smug satisfaction knowing she has taken the bait whether she wants to or not.

Idalia is bound to make the leap one way or another. We can't risk the fury of Fate. The sooner she's caught the safer we will all be.

Janice stands raising his mug of ale to the entire banquet hall, "A toast to my brethren in captivity. May we be thankful for our feast and *dear friends* to share it. Salute!"

"Salute!" A chorus rings throughout the hall. Idalia no longer able to bear the weight of loneliness in the midst of a taunting crowd downs her own mug before fleeing to find the nearest exit.

Conspiring eyes of the Fyre brethren following Idalia's hasty escape exchange knowing looks unaware of Narceous' many spies sitting amongst them. Some in their usual immortal form and others having shape shifted to blend seamlessly with their surroundings. A handful break away from the hall to follow her back to her quarters.

"Janice would see me banished to the mines!" Idalia cries out. She throws a chair against the far wall where it nearly disintegrates into a pile of splinters. Sobbing more from anger than misery she plants herself into her favorite chair wrapping herself in a large blanket.

Would the mines be any worse than this? Confined to the Citadel with nothing to do, not one true friend to confide in. Janice says my brethren are filled with sympathy for me. Lies. Besides, what good is sympathy? For that matter, what good are the Divine when they ignore my every plea. If only I knew how much longer Viktor would be gone. If only I could go back in time and talk Viktor out of approaching Gyntargh with his schemes. If, if, if...changes nothing.

What are my options? Keep the status quo where I slowly lose my mind or make a break for Earth to find Viktor. I choose the latter, but first my brethren must believe I've accepted our confinement.

While Idalia falls asleep plotting her supposed transformation of compliance Neilina feels her thinly veiled deception steadily growing. It's chilling shadow snakes through the halls like a slow-moving fog leaving a sense of foreboding doom in its wake.

THE LION & THE CRAB

Alicea relaxes with Viktor on their back patio under a beautiful clear blue sky. She watches her family of quail eating from the seed block she set out the night before.

Viktor pours a small glass of her favorite wine to go with a tray brimming over with a variety of cheese and fruits she'd prepared for them.

Alicea has been waiting for the perfect moment to broach the delicate subject of *socializing*. Yesterday she'd received the phone call Fianna had promised Nikolai. Sahana's gracious charismatic nature could not be denied. Alicea was more than excited at the prospect of Nikolai having friends not to mention she was long overdue for a friend herself.

"Viktor—" she pauses unsure where to start.

"Yes Love. What is on your mind this morning?"

Nervously, Alicea lets her words pour out in flood fashion, "We received an invitation from the aunt of one of Nikolai's friends to attend a birthday party—in fact, she mentioned the two of them have birthdays one day apart and offered to combine their birthdays so all their friends could attend together."

"Aunt? And what is this friend's name?"

"Fianna, the pretty red headed girl he's been playing basketball with lately. I believe they've also been spending time at a nearby bookstore."

Can it be Fianna of the Fyre? Viktor hopes in vain. It must be. What are the odds another child—living in the middle of the desert and going to the same school with a birthday one day apart—holds the same unusual name.

"And the aunt, what is her name?" he asks nonchalantly filling her plate full of cheese.

"Sahana, such a pretty name. I don't think I've ever heard that name before. Have you?"

"I think I have, somewhere in my many travels." Viktor recognizes the name as one of Agrimony's favorite brethren.

I'd hoped it would be awhile longer before I heard it again. As I recall she never did like me. Hmph, I don't like the old me either so who can blame her.

"I'm hoping you'll say yes. Nikolai is finally coming out of his shell," Alicea takes hold of his hand, "Viktor, children need socializing with their friends."

He looks into the face of the mortal woman who quite effortlessly captured his heart. Often, he pondered who'd chiseled the ice off his soul first, Alicea or Nikolai. He cherished each moment with them knowing they'd not be his forever.

"I suppose it is time," a sadness fills his soul, "Time—if I were its master, I'd slow it to a crawl."

Alicea reaches over to kiss his cheek, "Thank you! I'm going to call her back right now." Alicea picks up her cell tapping in Sahana's number, "Hello, Sahana. We love your idea for the birthday party! What can I do to help?"

From inside the house Nikolai stands in the kitchen frozen with shock listening to the party plans unfolding. A full ten minutes passes before he accepts the inevitable. Visualizing Fianna's triumphant smile he feels a growing irritation at his own miscalculation, but a picture of her flashes through his mind.

Sea green eyes in a sun kissed face sparkle with secrets wordlessly contrived as her laughter fills his senses.

Of course, her laughter normally comes after she's either insulted me or bested me at something. A small price for my ego to pay for her irresistible company. I can already see her look of satisfaction when we show up. She's too prideful. As am I.

Nikolai's posture relaxes, a smile slowly warms his violet eyes, and he reaches for his wallet. From between the rich leather folds he pulls out a crisp twenty-dollar bill. A quiet chuckle escapes as he tucks it back in his wallet reserving it for Fianna.

A subtle breeze makes its way through an open window bringing a summer garden's scent with it. Nikolai leans against the counter wondering if flowers would make a good birthday present for Fianna.

Alicea finds him deep in thought, "Nikolai I've wonderful news," Nikolai chooses not to spoil her surprise, "We're going to celebrate you and Fianna's birthday together this weekend and all your new friends will be there!"

"Wow, how did you pull that one off!"

"Are you happy? I mean, I thought..."

"Yes, I'm happy. Fianna's a good friend."

Alicea feels a flood of relief since she'd gambled the outcome without asking first, "That's a relief, I just want you to have a few special days to remember. You're growing up too fast and one day you'll be leaving for college."

"I know and I am grateful for all you do. Right now, I could actually do with a bit of your advice."

"You want my advice? About what?"

"I was thinking of flowers for Fianna's gift, but she's not like other girls so...."

"Flowers are always nice, but maybe paired with something more personal. Don't forget every flower symbolizes something—do a little internet search before you buy. Is there anything she's mentioned in the past, something she wants or needs? Maybe an out of the usual everyday trinket. You're a clever boy, you'll think of something," Alicea gives him one more hug then heads back to the patio.

Clever? Yes, but it would take a wizard to know Fianna's mind. Hmm, sports equipment? No, everyone will be thinking the obvious. An unusual trinket, but where to look? Ah, yes. I know.

***

Nikolai leans over a glass top display case in *Books & Brew* looking over the packed case of jewels, watches, and what-nots.

"Good morning Nikolai," Ms. O'Shea always greets Nikolai like family, "You've perfect timing, here try my newest beverage concoction," she hands him a small glass of a special dark tea. Nikolai drinks without hesitation, "Excellent, I'd take seconds if you have more."

"Sorry, that was my only sample."

"Lucky me, you must have seen me coming," Nikolai jokes.

As a matter of fact, I did.

"What brings you in this morning?"

"I'm hoping you have an unusual trinket for Fianna."

Before Niamh can answer Nikolai finds the treasure he seeks, "Never mind, I found it." He points to a small object in the far corner of the case. Ms. O'Shea places it in his hand and he knows it was meant for Fianna.

Huh, I guess Wizard be thy name.

"I don't suppose you gift wrap."

"Not normally, but for you I'll make an exception."

Nikolai was already blocks away with his wrapped gift when Fianna waited patiently for Niamh to finish wrapping her gift for Nikolai. She tipped her cup of brew upside down licking the last trickle.

I hope Ms. O'Shea has more of this next time Nikolai and I come back. Her teas are definitely GOAT. Never had anything like them before. Never would have guessed I'd like tea this much. Crazy.

"Here you are my dear."

"Thanks, see you next week."

The shop door closes with the tinkling of its hanging bell. As if on cue Lady Luck shimmers into view. Her form materializes standing at the door watching Fianna depart. She spins around smiling with both arms flourishing a touch down, "Who says oil and water can't mix?"

A laughing Maebh saunters down from the upstairs, "Certainly not the Mystics, we never doubted you for a moment."

"Your special recipe certainly helped today," Niamh tosses Fianna's empty cup in the waste basket.

Destiny chimes in from afar, "Not that anyone's asked, but it was I who arranged the time portal for Fianna's arrival placing her and Nikolai's arrival one day apart while taking advantage of planetary movement through the twelve houses."

"Yes, well done sister. Props to you. Their astrological arrival dates have certainly influenced them as much as their immortal heritage—at least while on Earth. Aren't you the clever one?" Fortune's smile fades a bit with realization it was not her talents alone overcoming the children's inherent tendency to squabble.

Both children entered Earth's Plane on the Leo/Cancer astrological cusp. While Nikolai's specific astrological date was not planned by Viktor it did fall within a water sign—Cancer—as well as the cusp of Leo thereby allowing Destiny the opportunity to send Fianna through the astrological time portal for Leo—a fire sign within the cusp of Cancer—at the same time other planets passing through specific houses would help bond them despite being polar opposites..

"Now sister, don't pout. You've performed your own miracles with them. After all, they are still souls of Fyre and Merbatho. Your special teas and trinkets serve them well. Keep up the good work. Fate is quite impressed."

"Don't worry. I've dug in and I'm here to see this ridiculous game to the end. You know I'd never walk away from a challenge," Fortune smiles brilliantly before vanishing with a spectacular display of swirling colors.

PATH SEEKERS

Alicea and Sahana agree to have the double birthday party at the park to accommodate the children's many friends. Nearly all of Fianna's friends from her track and basketball teams along with Nikolai's friends from his basketball and debate teams fill one of the park's covered picnic area. Friends and family line either side of a large picnic table piled high with gifts.

Fianna is first to open presents. She purposely waits to open Nikolai's present until last. A large birthday bag holds more than a couple presents. Her first and second boxes contain miscellaneous camping supplies for their inevitable summer journey. Over the top of the last box a red ribbon wraps around a small yellow rose symbolizing friendship. She recognizes the gold box and ribbon from *Books & Brew.* Drawing out the suspension for their friends, knowing they've all been side betting on the true nature of she and Nikolai's friendship, she slowly unwraps the yellow rose, lifting it she takes in its amazing perfume, "Mmm, that has got to be the best smell ever. Gunning to get your Jackson back, eh?"

She passes the rose around to her girlfriends who quickly confirm her senses do not lie, leaving a few girls feeling a bit envious while several boys make mental notes.

Next, she carefully opens the silver box anxious to reveal its treasure. Beneath a layer of soft gold tissue paper lies a short gold chain holding an oval peridot, her birthstone. Hanging below the gemstone is a small locket engraved with abstract lines running crosswise. She opens the locket to find a compass. The compass pulls her in much like the key that already hangs from her neck to lie hidden beneath her shirt. Holding it up for all to see there is a great deal of oohing and awing from the girls.

"Here let me put it on you," Nikolai moves in close wrapping his arms around her neck to fasten the clasp. Several friends quietly grin and elbow each other.

"Thank you, it's beautiful," she says loudly for the whole group, "I think you'll like my present as well," Fianna whispers for Nikolai alone to hear.

Although intrigued Nikolai also saves her present for last. He opens his many gifts hoping he's showing the correct amount of gratitude. Truly grateful for his friends' efforts, some more successful than others, he wants all to know his appreciation is sincere.

Last but by no means least, he finally comes to Fianna's gift pile. He too recognizes a special box in the mix. The first box contains a couple small geodes and some of his favorite gemstones. The second box contains a small leather wrist band with a pair of crossed arrows carved in it; a symbol for best friends. Slipping it over his wrist he murmurs in her ear, "*Best* friends, you one upped me again." Fianna smiles with great affection sans her usual smugness.

Viktor and Sahana stand on opposite sides of the table mystified as to how these two immortal children had grown so fond of one another. The young Fyre and Merbatho children generally mix no better than oil and water. Viktor and Sahana suspect outside influence—of the Divine sort. Alicea already thrilled to see Nikolai surrounded by so many friends is over the moon seeing he has a special friend in Fianna.

The crowd goes eerily silent when Nikolai reaches for the silver box. The treasure lies beneath glossy silver paper. Nikolai carefully removes the paper. A blue velvet interior showcases a short silver chain nestled in the middle with a diamond shaped ruby attached. He pulls it slowly from the velvet to show the silent crowd. Hanging below the ruby is a mirror image of Fianna's locket.

"Synchronicity!" Nikolai and Fianna revel in the moment.

They high five each other sealing their secret alliance to soon depart in search for that which calls them each night through cosmic dreams of fire and ice.

A befuddled look spreads across the faces of two immortals standing six feet apart. Alicea elbows Viktor as she claps and congratulates the children. Viktor grasps Alicea's cue and follows suit congratulating and thanking the appropriate people all the while his mind stumbles down the same path as Sahana's. It feels as though a glorious puzzle hangs in front of them with just enough missing pieces to obscure the picture. One of many questions springs forth in both their minds.

Who's holding the missing pieces?

"Viktor, would you mind if I go to Fianna's house for a couple hours. We're comparing some of our geological maps for a research project we've been working on," Nikolai interrupts Viktor's internal dialogue.

"Research? During summer break?"

"It's our personal project. We've a common interest in ley lines and vortexes."

"Oh, I suppose if her aunt doesn't mind."

"It's fine, I already asked days ago."

Sahana gives an approving nod from across the table before turning to answer another parent's question.

"Be home before dark," Viktor orders with utmost seriousness.

"And text me when you're leaving Fianna's place, okay?" Alicea chimes in with her usual overprotective mode.

"Will do," Nikolai hugs Alicea as she gathers up all his presents with the exception of the locket that hangs a few inches above his hidden key.

Viktor sighs watching Nikolai walk away with Fianna. He's never seen the boy look so happy.

I wonder how long their camaraderie will last now that they've entered the Contest's playing field. Many an ancient immortal has been broken having fallen in defeat upon similar fields.

Sahana also watches their departure. The two walk mere inches apart with heads bent towards one another conspiring in hushed voices.

'Synchronicity' they did shout. I wonder what secrets those two share so easily? Have they already come to suspect a joint venture draws close? How can they know what lies ahead? Destiny, I beg the Divine keep them safe.

***

"Come on up to my room and I'll show you mine," Fianna races up the stairs, flings the bedroom door wide open and motions Nikolai in. Her map stares him in the face—all six feet of it.

"Um—yeah. My map is a bit more scaled down, but we can still work out the logistics." He unrolls his own short scroll. Intuitively he senses Fianna awaits his approval.

"Your work is amazing. Every single vortex listed in our research is pinned. You've also marked nearby landmarks."

"Yeah, I have and now," she opens a drawer pulling out red twine and stickpins, "we can overlay it with your ley lines."

"It feels as if we're in a boat being pulled down river by a strong current—without a paddle," Nikolai awaits Fianna's assessment.

"True, but for me it's too late to turn back now."

"My dreams are filled with symbols I've never seen, people I've never met, and all we've learned yet still needs piecing together. I'm in it to the end."

"Thus, into the unknown we sail," Fianna dramatically unravels her red twine.

SHOES THAT BETRAY

Idalia's calculated efforts to convince her brethren she's moved on from Viktor have convinced the majority, but Neilina and Narceous remain suspicious of her every move. She feels Neilina's eyes on her from the Citadel's every corner.

I think it may be time for me to expand my circle of friends. I wonder what those in the Erthen Citadel are up to. A walk through the Square of Commons sounds harmless enough.

Idalia makes her way through the banquet hall smiling when appropriate, looking everyone square in the eye as she does and without even the slightest hint of subterfuge.

"Greetings Idalia," Janice calls from his usual crowd filled table with only a few eyes turning towards her.

"Greetings, are we still meeting for a late banquet at your place?"

"Absolutely, I'm breaking out my best ale just for you!" Janice flashes a wide toothy smile—his hallmark sign of a lie.

"I'll be looking forward to it!" Idalia counters Janice's theatrical lie with an enthusiastic lying smile of her own while mentally throwing knives at his teeth.

A few more gracious smiles for her brethren and she is out the door heading for the SOC. Two of Neilina's team start after her, but hang back when she takes a bench within the SOC.

"What do we do now?" asks a lower ranking guard.

"Nothing. Our orders state the Guard is to keep constant surveillance on her within every room of the

Citadel. She has left the Citadel. Stay here and report if she crosses back onto Fyre grounds."

Idalia monitors the guards from their reflection in a garden window.

Neilina's guards standing down. Huh, wasn't expecting that.

She sits a few moments listening to the conversations milling about her. A couple argues over what to plant in their garden, another argue over disciplining a young immortal, a couple of off duty guards from the Fyre Citadel discuss how to improve the procedures for the *changing of the guard* which happens four times a day. Their ensuing conversation gives Idalia an idea.

Making her way casually around the square's perimeter she stands at the corner of a hedge towering on the Fyre border. She pretends to inspect a small bird nesting in the foliage. Taking a hard glance about the square she ascertains there are only five of the Fyre within the square including the two guards.

Setting one foot behind her, she takes a final glance, spins on her heel and disappears behind the hedge where a path lies between the tall thick hedge and its twin creating a path that circles the Fyre Citadel.

Peeking through a small opening in the interior hedge she finds servants folding clean laundry. Pulling an orange cloak from a nearby basket she wraps herself in it hiding beneath its hood. Several immortals pass by paying her no heed until one goddess happens to notice Idalia's shoes. Shoes of a warrior are never worn with the cloak of a servant much less one assigned to the rooms of the highest rank—Neilina's rooms. The goddess says nothing waiting to distance herself from the imposter. She comes to where the corridor breaks open and runs to the entry guards. She gives description of the imposter.

Meanwhile Idalia has made it to the rear entrance. It is almost time for the new guard to come on duty. She waits patiently ignorant of the detailed description the guards are hearing at the front entrance.

Finally! Taking a deep breath to steady her nerves when the new guard appears, she watches closely finally grasping the flaws of their procedure.

Traffic through this entrance is unimpeded as the guards turn to one another to salute and exchange reports.

Idalia leaves the corridor slipping by the guards easily enough. Making her way through the back entrance puts her closest to the lower portals. They won't get her to the third plane, but that isn't her initial destination. Quickly clearing the distance to one of these portals her hand reaches from beneath the cloak to open a portal. Idalia's racing heart pounds in her ears muffling the commotion of advancing guards rushing through the citadel's many corridors with their doors opening only to be quickly slammed shut as the all-out hunt for a cloaked intruder draws closer. She deftly opens her door to freedom, slips through before its half opened, and silently closes it. The cloak's hood falls to her shoulders, feverish eyes squint in the dim light searching for a small round pad—the palm of her hand skims across its quartz center. Idalia's form instantly apparates to pure energy leaving the orange cloak lying on the floor.

High above in the tallest towers a gloom filled Neilina perches on the edge of a chair, elbows resting on knees with clasped hands, guards pound furiously on the door before bursting in, "We've reports of an impostor dressed as one of your personal servants. You're in danger!"

"You're too late. She's already escaped," Neilina states matter of fact. The shift in the Citadel's energy when Idalia's energy left the Fifth Plane pierced the veil of deceit she'd felt hanging about the castle. Add to that, the opening of a citadel's portal is always felt by the citadel's highest member. Neilina put the two together immediately.

"What do we do now?" asks a confused guard.

"Return to your posts and wait for the sign."

"Sign—what sort of sign?"

"Judgement. The sign of judgment." Neilina lets her head fall into her hands in defeat. She awaits Fate's fury.

TREACHEROUS TIMES

"Dear Neilina, your defeat is only in your mind," Destiny's been monitoring Idalia—as she does all beings under her watch—wondering which path she would choose. Disappointed but not surprised she must now show her sister Fate.

Finding Fate in a deep state of meditation she uses to monitor all souls on various planes. Her form is transparent yet glows with fluctuating colors as she sees all. In her present state she communicates telepathically with Destiny.

Destiny, you worry needlessly. I am aware of the Fyre warrior's deeds, and Neilina will not be held responsible for Idalia's treachery. Send our Little Mischief to deal with Idalia.

Destiny nods her head in acknowledgment and returns to her chamber of portals to locate her sister still on the Fifth Plane.

Meanwhile, Fortune smiles on Fianna and Nikolai as they correlate their two maps putting the pieces together—literally. Nikolai sits at Fianna's desk, with scraps of his former map strewn around him, he carefully cuts a square from a small scrap of his map.

"This is the last one," Nikolai hands Fianna a small square with ley lines and landmarks.

Fianna pins it to the corresponding landmark on her own map, "That should do it, but now what?"

"Now we plot a course."

"Duh—obviously. I meant where should we start first? Should we pick the nearest landmark and go from there?"

"I was thinking of synchronicity. Perhaps our compasses will help?" Nikolai pulls his compass and key from beneath his shirt. Fianna follows suit.

"Let's open them together," Fianna sits on the bed facing Nikolai, "Okay, one, two, three!" Lockets open simultaneously.

"Mine is just spinning," Fianna scowls.

"Mine too."

"Maybe they're broke," Fianna's voice full of disappointment.

"We should go ask Ms. O'Shea if there's a place to fix them."

"Plus, we need to see if that last book came in," the needle on the compasses suddenly springs to the northwest, "Did your needle just move too?"

Nikolai checks his compass, "Yes, it's pointing northwest."

"Same here. Mine jumped when I mentioned the book. What's northwest?"

"*Books and Brew.* I don't think our compasses are broke."

"Me either. First thing tomorrow then?"

"Definitely," Nikolai checks the time on his cell phone, "I better get going or Alicea will be calling out a search party."

Fianna walks Nikolai downstairs. As their chattering fades Fortune stands in front of the desk scrutinizing their new map. She's adjusting a few of the ley lines in relation to the landmarks when she feels the familiar pull to the Divine Plane.

"Honestly, what now?" She vanishes from the room leaving the map almost perfect—almost.

***

Destiny feels roiling energy entering the Seventh Plane, "*Someone's* in a mood!" The sound of crackling lightening echoes through her chamber, "Enough of the theatrics my Little Mischief. You've been called back to hunt down an immortal who's broken a Divine Order."

Fortune materializes with a pop, "Ugh, the immortals are becoming more troublesome than humans—is it arrogance or mere stupidity?"

"It is irrelevant. Now come and see," Destiny turns the Fifth Plane's wheel of time stopping it at the banquet when Janice first baited Idalia. Fortune takes in Idalia's schemes sees where she jumped from the Fourth Dimension onto the Third Plane's wheel of time then shooting through the Earth's first house—the house of ego and self-interest.

"Self-serving piece of work, isn't she?" Fortune's tone turns chilly, "Where is she now?"

Destiny moves fast forwards the wheel aligning it with Idalia's energy, "She has found Viktor's home. You must hurry for when his true love is revealed. Alicea may be in danger."

Roiling with contempt Fortune vanishes to reappear as blue jay perched high in a tree looking down on Idalia hiding behind a well-trimmed hedge.

What have we here? A foolish immortal looking more rabbit than warrior. How dare she defy Fate's Order!

Too weak to conquer the darkness that feeds her ego, but now here she stands at a fork between two paths gifting her a choice. Destiny, you are ever hopeful.

The time to choose is granted. A choice to walk away with her grief or dive into the pool of revenge—though she will never even touch the waters. Look at her thinking herself the hunter in hiding. Oh tiny prey, your ignorance shall be fleeting if I have my way.

Idalia spies Viktor gazing out a window deep in thought, "My poor love. What agony of boredom you have endured stuck on this rock where time crawls too slowly," her immortal heart cries out to him. Rising from her hiding place she is suddenly frozen in place. Alicea has joined Viktor at the window. Pure adoration pours from his eyes as he leans in to kiss her.

What is this treachery? I've risked all for him! Our love was a hoax. I was never anything to him!

The searing pain of a cold betrayal washes over Idalia. The weight of it pushing her back down into the hedge to weep silently. Several minutes pass before the weeping quite suddenly comes to a halt. Hands dripping with scalding tears fall away from her face. Not a trace of sadness lingers in her stone-cold face. Fierce eyes turn to the sky burning with a hunger. A hunger for revenge. Idalia vanishes silently into thin air.

And there we have it! Fortune readies to capture her prey.

Patience, she has yet to act. Her path has not yet solidified. Give her more time. You are to keep an eye on her for now. Her actions will determine the severity of punishment.

Destiny stays Fortune's hand and the irate blue jay puffs herself into a feathery ball of fluff before vanishing to follow Idalia.

***

Sunday morning Niamh greets Fianna and Nikolai as they enter her store, "Good morning, your book arrived yesterday afternoon. Speaking of…how was your birthday party?"

"It was lit! Half the school showed up. Everybody loved our compasses." Fianna pulls hers out to admire it following Niamh to their special corner of the store.

Niamh hands Nikolai a book from the coffee table, "Here you go. I left the other three books from the author out on the table for you. Thought you might need them."

"Thanks Ms. O'Shea, we appreciate all your help," Nikolai offers his genuine gratitude.

"You're welcome, as always." Niamh leaves them to their discoveries.

Nikolai grabs the other three books as they sit down. He places them face up with the fourth book. Fianna's head turns side to side staring at the books, "Is it my imagination or is there a cipher between the four covers?" She points to different corners of the covers, each having a tiny intricate design.

Nikolai is in disbelief, "How did I not see it all this time?"

"What is it?" Fianna having turned all four books so that the meeting of the designs finally form a true picture.

"I know what it is. More importantly, what does it mean?"

PREPARATIONS

"You *know* this symbol? That figures," Fianna scowls.

"Do you want to know what it is or not?"

"You do know my ego gets another bruise every time you beat me to the punch? But go ahead, you were saying?"

"I was going to point out that this symbol is actually comprised of two separate symbols. See the outer portion is a Celtic braid encircling this inner portion," Nikolai points to the interior symbol, "it's known as Metatron's cube. Look at the lines connecting across the full picture now."

"You're right! Apart they resembled some sort of abstract art on each of the individual covers..."

"But now they totally make sense," Nikolai echoes Fianna's trailing thought.

"Ley lines," the two whisper in awe.

"What do ley lines, vortexes, crystals, and the cipher all have in common?" Nikolai pauses to let Fianna work the out the puzzle.

"Energy," puzzle solved and answered in seconds, "but how do the keys and compass fit in?"

"I have a feeling—no, more of a push—to see these vortexes in person. We'll find answers there, I'm sure of it. Maybe not all of them, but it's a start."

"We should investigate some of the closer megaliths too."

"Agreed. But before we can consider all of that, we have to convince Viktor and Sahana to let us go," Nikolai is ninety-nine percent sure Viktor will say yes. He's not so sure about Sahana.

"We'll finish reading this new book, break for lunch, request a meeting with them both, then present a mature logical analysis of the possible learning opportunities in our trip. You should let me do the talking."

"And if that doesn't work?"

"Trust me. It'll work."

"Hold on, we've forgotten our tea and cookies." Nikolai jumps to pile cookies high on a tiny plate while Fianna fills two glasses with Niamh's latest concoction.

Maebh watches from her crystal ball upstairs, "Hmph, they solved their first puzzle without any help. Tsk, a waste of a perfectly charmed tea.

"No, not a waste at all. I can feel the charm is heavily active, and since it was cast with the intent to fizzle out once its purpose was served..." Rionach assures her granddaughter as she turns the page of a magazine, "it's work is not yet finished."

Rionach sighs, "You know I think, when our duties end here, I'll take a trip to the Emerald Isle."

"It's too gorgeous. Your first incarnation on the Third Plane, yes?"

"Yes, it was. And it made a lasting impression. Quite different now, but it always feels like home."

***

After lunch Nikolai and Fianna made their calls. All parties agree to meet at *Books and Brew* so Fianna could use the research books in her analysis of what they'd learned and what's yet to be learned.

Fianna and Nikolai stand looking down on the two immortals torn with the knowledge they are about to lose their charges to the contest. Foresight having improved,

Viktor left Alicea at home with the pretense Nikolai wasn't feeling well enough to walk home.

"And in conclusion, we feel experiencing the vortexes ourselves is crucial in furthering our research. How can we explain it to our friends and teachers if we merely give other people's opinions and claims? We want to *know*," Fianna nervously concludes her analysis. She failed to anticipate the degree of Viktor's presence in their cramped study corner.

Well, say something!

Viktor, feeling equally nervous, sits stone still contemplating the safety of Nikolai and Fianna. What dangers lie in wait for them? He wished fervently he could follow them if only to keep them safe. He wished he could say no. But it was not within his power.

"Well, that is quite the presentation," Sahana breaks the uncomfortable silence.

"Yes. Yes, it is. When were you planning on leaving and how will you be traveling?" Viktor breaks from his internal fretting.

"I thought perhaps we could take the truck with the ATV in the bed for any rough off roads we might encounter," Nikolai had planned on broaching the subject when they were home again.

"Wise decision. Always be prepared." Viktor praises his forethought.

"We're hoping to leave in three days, be gone ten days, then head back," Fianna's voice confident in their choices, "We also want to try and locate any ley lines running through Arizona."

"As well as take a tour through a gem stone mine that's open to the public," Nikolai's enthusiasm grows by the minute.

"Then I suppose we'd better go shopping for some hiking attire and supplies," Sahana manages to speak despite the lump in her throat.

"Really?" Fianna's triumphant squeal sets Viktor chuckling.

"We are ready and at your service," Viktor turns to Sahana, "and you as well. Let me know if there is anything we can help with."

"Thank you," Sahana knows Viktor's hidden meaning refers to keeping them safe and protected. He is not the same demigod who stole the boy out of heartless ignorance and greed. She knows he'd give his own life for the boy if it comes down to it.

"Excuse me, but I couldn't help overhearing your plans. I wanted to offer your favorite books as reference guides on your trip," Niamh motions to the four small books on the coffee table.

"Thank you. Fianna takes great notes, but you never know what will come in handy," Nikolai is relieved for the offer and he would not have to ask for the borrow of them.

Niamh picks the books up. Stacking them in a particular order she stretches a braided band around the small stack. The small stack of books beam brighter as she hands them to Nikolai.

"You really are the best Ms. O'Shea," Fianna throws her long arms around her neck for a hug. Fianna steps back flashing her prettiest smile shining with pure joy.

In that moment Viktor sees it. Family resemblance—the resemblance to her mother, Narceous. He shudders wondering what horrors she's been scheming in his honor.

***

Fianna and Nikolai each lie in their beds on their cell phones debating their options for motel, food, and finally their time of departure. Destination—Sedona, Arizona.

"Okay, I just locked in my reservation," Fianna yawns as she stares at campground reservation on her cell phone.

Nikolai's voice comes over the speaker phone, "Me too. How do you feel about packing the truck tomorrow?"

"After lunch works for me. Sahana and I will be shopping all morning."

"Okay, that will give me time to read through this last. We kind of flew through it the first time around."

"Yeah we did. Let me know if you find anything helpful or interesting. I gotta get some sleep now, goodnight."

"Will do, goodnight." Nikolai soon falls into uneasy dreams.

LETTING GO

Nightmares filled with pictures of people and places Nikolai has never seen before finally cease shortly before sunrise. One blurry face in particular leaves him uneasy. While many of the images passing through his dreams looked out of focus, a pair of eyes loomed out from the sea of murky faces. Clear as daylight, their burning need for vengeance shook Nikolai to his core.

Ugh, I need coffee and a shower.

Viktor finds him an hour later in the kitchen. A spoonful of cereal in one hand and book *four* in the other.

"You're up early," Nikolai jumps at Viktor's baritone voice. His spoonful of cereal lands on the kitchen table. Viktor's rising eyebrow questions the moment as he tosses a kitchen towel, "Clean up on aisle ten? Since when do I get the jump on you?"

"Since I barely slept."

"More coffee," Viktor holds up the coffee pot.

"Most definitely, thank you."

"What's on your agenda today?" Viktor eyes the small book in Nikolai's hand with about twenty pages left unread.

"Fianna's shopping this morning—then we're packing the truck after lunch," Nikolai never looks up from his book.

I don't remember reading this! Nikolai turns the book over to check the cover and title. *Yep, it's the right book. Huh, we must have skipped over this chapter.*

Viktor places his hand over the book's cover. Nikolai looks up to see him smiling, "See you at lunch, I've some shopping as well. Grabbing his travel mug, he lumbers on his way briefly stopping at the front door, "By the way, we're hosting dinner tonight for Fianna and her aunt. No, don't thank me, it's all Alicea's doing," Viktor leaves with a chuckle. Reaching for the door of his Jag he stops short. Sensing a familiar energy—generously laced with venom—he whispers, "Idalia?"

Scanning the nearby hedges, knowing them to be her favorite camouflage, he watches the trailing remnants of her energy fade away. Ignorant of her true intentions and circumstances he's eager for news from the Fyre. He speeds away hoping she will follow.

Five miles down the road, any outside observer would assume the Jag experienced a slight bump in the road. Instead, behind the darkly tinted windows Idalia sits glaring daggers at Viktor.

"Idalia! What are *you* doing here, where's Gyntargh, has something happened?"

Idalia's venom recedes a micron, "Has no one told you?"

"Told me what? I've neither seen nor heard from anyone in the Fyre since I left."

Idalia's insane laughter fills the Jag's small interior. Viktor's aggravation grows exponentially. Idalia's humor turns viciously smug, "Let me fill in the blanks for you, my *dear* Viktor."

***

Alicea hands the day's trash bag to Viktor with a kiss on his cheek, "Thank you, sweetheart." She resumes the nightly chore of kitchen duty with Sahana's help. Viktor takes the bag of refuse out the back door to a garbage can in the alley.

Nikolai and Fianna, enjoying the rare exemption from K-duty, sit on the floor in the den surrounded by their research books, notes, and loose hard copies printed from the internet. Their combined map of vortexes and ley lines lie rolled out before them with each of them holding one end of the large scroll.

"Did you finish reviewing book *four* like you wanted?"

"I did. Do you remember reading a chapter about multiple ley lines crossing vortexes—-as in more than just a couple?"

"No. Why?"

"I think we skipped a chapter the first time we read it."

"Well, Ms. O'Shea's cookies are a distraction," Fianna jokes.

"You should read it again while I drive. There's more."

"Like what?"

"A map with Metatron's cube overlaying vortexes with multiple ley lines passing through them."

"Near Sedona?"

"No, the southeast and the Atlantic Ocean."

"Wow," she whispers, "What are the chances we could get a combo summer vacay this year?"

"Viktor would take us. He loves to travel.

Outside, Viktor shuts the alley gate behind him, turns and nearly runs into Idalia.

"My, my—the legendary warrior taking out trash like a common servant. How the mighty have fallen."

"Idalia. I've made my apologies now return to the Fifth Plane."

"Are you kidding? Who would watch over the kiddies on their road trip? Certainly not you or Sahana. No breaking the rules for you two—not to mention your little pet might get hurt."

"Touch one hair on my Alicea and I'll deliver you to Neilina myself!" Viktor growls ferociously.

"That's more like it. I knew the old Viktor was still lurking somewhere inside you. Unfortunately, I can't stay to reminisce. I've mayhem to plot and a road trip to wreck—literally," Idalia vanishes leaving her insane laugh to linger behind.

***

Nikolai and Fianna wave as they pull out of the driveway. Alicea wipes away a tear shouting, "Be careful, stay safe!"

Sahana waves goodbye with one eye on Viktor and the other watching for trouble. She sensed Idalia's energy when leaving the dinner party.

Something has changed. Viktor looks as though he's about to go supernova. Fortune, please—let us watch over the children!

A breeze rustles her hair whispering in her ear, "It is not your path to take. Stay your course for I am with them. No harm shall come to them."

Sahana's instantaneous relief washes over Viktor. He spies her out of the corner of his eye. Her relaxed body language reassures him a Divine power keeps their treasures safe.

Nikolai and Fianna head north to Sedona with the wind at their backs, full of optimism, and completely unaware they're dead center in the cross hairs of a vengeful immortal trailing close behind.

***

Nikolai awakes late the next morning. He texts Fianna from his own tent.

N: You awake yet?
F: No. duh, of course I am. Let's get on the road.
N: Putting my shoes on now.
F: Sweet let's go!

Nikolai exits his tent with a duffle bag full of breakfast snacks over his shoulder and two bars in his hand.

Fianna grabs a bar from him, "We're about a half hour from Red Rock," she takes a bite of the bar as she hops in the truck, "Chocolate chips, my fav!"

"I remembered," Nikolai jumps into the driver's seat and tosses the duffle in the back seat. He drives them back to the main road.

"I don't remember which direction I turned last night."

"Let's check our compasses, they should point the way. Mine says to go straight."

"Mine too," Nikolai confirms the strange directions, "What does that sign over there say?"

"West Forks Hiking Trail. Hmm, I think I printed a guide for that trail. Shall we try it?"

Nikolai pulls across the road to the self-pay for parking, "Sure, what's the worst that could happen?"

THE STORYTELLER

Fianna studies the hiking guide for the West Forks Trail, "Looks like this trail is about three miles long."

"I can't help but wonder if there is a vortex here that's not shown on any of our maps."

"Or ley lines maybe," Fianna glances at their stack of research material in the back seat.

Nikolai points to the map's legend, "It's labeled an easy trail, but I think we should take our time. The compasses sent us here for a reason."

"Sounds weird, 'The compasses sent us'...kind of freaks me out." Fianna folds the map into her pocket.

"Me too. You know—I've been having weird dreams this past week. Nightmares some nights."

"Fuzzy pictures of people and places you don't recognize? Me too."

"And worse. Want to turn back?" Nikolai waits patiently as Fianna considers this strange path they share, "You don't have to do this."

"No, I don't. But I have to know where all of this leads," she holds up the compass and key dangling around her neck, "These came to us both, we both have similar dreams, we both feel the pull to some unseen force or object or place—I don't what it is. But it feels closer every day." She lets them fall from her hand where the morning sunshine dances over them.

Nikolai nods his head in agreement, "We've come too far to turn back. No matter what lies at the end of our path we will meet it together." Nikolai pulls his compass and key from beneath his shirt wearing them as badges of bravery.

Fianna lifts the palm of her hand towards him, "Let's do this!" Nikolai high fives her, "Onward we come and fear we've none!"

***

"From my calculations we should be nearly at the end of the trail," Fianna points to a landmark on her map as they continue walking, "We've reached the tall canyon walls and they're starting to close in on us."

"Yeah, and it appears the other hikers have turned around."

"My compass insists we continue on. See the needle is vibrating."

Nikolai stops suddenly grabbing Fianna's arm, "Someone is ahead of us on the other side of those rocks."

"And waiting *for us*."

"You feel it too?"

"Yes, and I have to admit—fear has taken my breath away," Fianna's voice shrinks to barely audible.

"Take as long as you need."

A breeze gently caresses their faces before whispering, "Do not be afraid children for Fortune smiles upon you this day. Be brave."

Nikolai looks at Fianna, "You hear that?"

Fianna takes a gulp of air, nods her head, and slowly moves forward. With curiosity in full bloom they proceed cautiously. Nikolai keeps his step close while quietly singing.

A winding path this day we tread
Stray away? No, we'd never!
This winding path we cautiously tread

"So much for 'fear we've none'", Fianna's laugh hinges ever so lightly on the edge of hysteria.

***

On the other side of the bend a tall, hooded figure is watching and waiting. Nikolai and Fianna round the bend walking along the pebbled beach that trims the revenants of the dwindling creek.

Finally, how slow can they be? Look at them. They smell more human than immortal. Fortune does indeed smile upon you, and though she has been quick to thwart my every attempt to land you upside down in a ditch, she cannot silence my words. A calamity upon your bodies I cannot commit, but I will and can open your minds to see that which has been hidden beneath those murky waters clouding up your dreams. May you now know your years of childhood to be nothing but lies. Pain borne of deceit— its revelation nearly two decades in the making shall be my revenge.

Idalia overhears Nikolai say, "Shall I do all the talking?" Fianna nods her head 'yes'.

Idalia's eyes fierce with vengeance belie the warm smile she attempts. The same eyes from Nikolai's nightmares sends shivers down his spine. *Fortune is with us. Be brave!*

"Hello," Nikolai greets the strange woman refusing to flinch from those eyes.

"Greetings, I am the Storyteller. I'm so glad you found your way to the end of the trail, too few do. I've stories to share of vortexes and ley lines, gods and goddesses, dream revealed, and most importantly— my stories are all true stories."

"We've come a long way to find such stories," Fianna's surprised by the sound of her voice.

"Follow me and have a seat. Make yourselves comfortable."

The fact she has deliberately placed them to the east of the stream and north of the too tiny campfire piques Fianna's curiosity.

Something I read long ago and now cannot remember. Ugh, I wish I had my notes. I suddenly fill like a piece in a puzzle.

"You've such interesting pendants," Idalia senses they are charmed for protection. She dares not touch them.

"We found these in a bookstore," Nikolai holds up his compass.

"Don't you mean—they found you?" Idalia asks pointedly.

"Um, how do you know that?" Fianna hopes she's allowed to ask.

"Because I too was once trapped in a web of synchronicity. Although, I was never blindfolded in ignorance of circumstances. I knew what I was getting into. In fact, I foolishly volunteered."

"Volunteered for what?" Nikolai unconsciously leans forward hanging on her every word.

***

"Another moral challenge this demigod will fail. I am not surprised. Idalia's moral compass has always pointed to her own self interests," Fate stands with Destiny staring with her down into the crystalline bowl. She turns from the bowl to watch Idalia and the children through the portal.

"True. Hmm, a new interesting path forms from her failure. One borne of empathy," Destiny staring into the bowl.

"Where, show me please."

"Right here, this tiny pink piece breaking off this red path that she currently sits upon. Color me shocked!" Destiny jokes sarcastically, "But she always returns to this red path," Destiny frowns in frustration.

"We must remember. Idalia is a demigod whose challenges come at her from two different worlds. That red path has saved her on more than one occasion."

Destiny considers Fate's words, "Discernment is what she needs. Knowing when to choose her red path…"

"…And when to abandon it," Fate finishes her sister's thought, "What has triggered this new path I wonder."

"Her own words," Destiny scrolls the portal backwards in time.

Because I too was once trapped in a web of synchronicity. Idalia's words reverberate until the pink path swims on its own.

Destiny's eyes smile, "Words, how they hold such power."

REVELATIONS

"For the same game you yourselves are unwittingly lost in... the *Contest for Conquest.* A game of the gods."

Nikolai and Fianna look at one another speechless. After a moment Nikolai finds his words, "We don't understand."

"And that's an understatement," Fianna looks incredulous, "We're plain everyday high school kids. What are we to gods?"

"You are children of the gods. Literally, you are one of the immortals. Fianna belongs to my brethren, the Fyre Gods. Nikolai, you belong to the Merbatho Gods. You have always felt different from this world you live in. Yet, here you are. And you must finish this game if you want to ever see your true home...your true family."

"No way," Fianna scoffs at the notion.

"You must think we're the most gullible kids on the planet," Nikolai feeling insulted by the idea alone scowls angrily at this stranger.

"I know you are not gullible. Your refusing to accept the truth does not change your reality. Fianna, you were raised by an immortal of the Fyre Citadel. And you Nikolai. You were raised by a demigod. Feel the truth of my words."

"I believe you," Fianna can barely whisper her acceptance.

"Yes, I feel the truth of your words. I feel as if an incredible weight has been thrown upon my shoulders," Nikolai's look of shock speaks volumes.

Now that she has their attention, Idalia continues explaining their lineage, their journey to the Third Plane, and their purpose in the game.

"Now, it's time for each of you to find your opponent's portal of entry. The one that leads directly to their Citadel. Fianna's key opens only the Merbatho's portal. Nikolai's opens only the Fyre's portal. You are players on opposite sides of game you cannot escape. The game is over when one of you unlocks the other's portal to home. It is the only way you can go home. And that—is the truth."

Nikolai and Fianna sit in a state of numbing shock with tears streaming silently from their eyes.

Idalia thought it would be her moment of triumphant revenge. The children's realization of their abandonment—to be raised under false pretense and all for a game to settle a dispute—contorts their beautiful faces in twisted pain. By her own words she has set herself upon a new path speaking aloud that which has uncovered and amplified her own buried pain. Her heart cries out shattering the black icy shell encasing her immortal heart for too many millenniums across too many galaxies.

"What have I done?" Idalia whispers to herself, "I've wielded the truth like a dagger to the heart—a child's heart—all to appease my own anger and pain?" Idalia breaks down sobbing, "Forgive me. Your story was not mine to tell. It was not the time for you to know and not this way. I am truly sorry," Idalia' sincere apology is heard and seen on both the Fifth Plane and the Divine.

"Divine forgiveness you have," a voice booms from behind a ridge of tall boulders. A hooded figure jumps down from a two-story boulder landing with a thud to tower over Idalia, "but the Divine will not speak for the children."

"Brahmal?"

"Yes, and I bring a message from Destiny. Brahmal lays his hand upon Idalia's shoulder, "It is time you return to your Fyre now."

"I will. I deserve whatever my punishment may be."

"You have punished yourself already. Now let yourself heal and learn from it. Neilina awaits your return."

Idalia takes one last look at the children through her tears, "You should have learned of this from another. I *am* sorry," Idalia's form fades then wavers to a wisp before quietly vanishing.

The sun sits almost at high noon, "Take out your keys and hold them to your third eye...here," Brahmal commands indicating on his own forehead. Nikolai and Fianna comply without question. "When the sun is at its apex a portal opens. Though it will not allow entry, you will see and be seen for the first time since you were taken from your true home

Nikolai and Fianna's keys begin to glow. Each creating its own bubble of light to encase the immortal who wields it. Each of them sees and hear their own brethren standing together cheering them onward to the finish line. Their families standing together at the forefront waving and calling out their names.

A torrential rain of early childhood memories from infancy flood in to fill the cores of Nikolai and Fianna. Family, nannies, and friends are recognized. An immortal's fervent desire to win the game for their own brethren and to return home overcomes each of them. But they are physically, mentally, and emotionally drained.

The portal to the citadels slowly closes and Destiny appears, "I am Destiny, one of three Divine Rulers. You are overwhelmed with exhaustion. Rest is needed before your new paths will solidify. I will return to visit again soon." She disappears and the bubble is gone.

Fianna looks up, licks her dry lips and swallows trying to find her voice, "This is a lot to take in. Nikolai?"

He sits frozen staring straight ahead, "Yeah. Still processing. Is this some kind of elaborate hoax?" His brilliant mind answers *no.*

Brahmal laughs, "No, and there's a few tricks you need to learn before we turn you loose. But first you must rest. Take my hand," He grabs a hand from each of them. In two blinks they are standing in front of their tents, "Rest your bodies, rest your minds, and when you are recovered Your training begins."

"My truck...oh, never mind," Nikolai sees his truck is already parked behind him. He and Fianna climb into their tents, kick off their shoes, and fall into a deep restful sleep.

At midnight Destiny returns. The children have recovered though they remain in a deep sleep under Brahmal's guard.

"Greetings Destiny of the Divine," Brahmal kneels.

"Greetings Brahmal, please rise. They will wake soon. You will explain today's brief training while they eat," a flourish of her hand produces a small tent with table, chairs, and two plates filled with a breakfast fit for an immortal, "training should begin immediately after breakfast. Fate has unbound their immortal powers. You will show them how, when, and where they may use them. Then return home. The Majix will be with them on the remainder of their journey."

"At your will," Brahmal reaffirms his obedience to the Divine as is customary.

"I will return before nightfall."

Destiny's regal form fades silently away with the morning breeze. Awakening immortal children break the quiet dawn with their yawning and stretching.

"Rise and shine, your breakfast is ready," Brahmal announces.

"Already rising," Nikolai exits his tent with a smile.

"And shining! I've never had such an awesome night's sleep," Fianna stands next to Nikolai looking ready to run a marathon.

"Sit. Eat, drink—and then we train."

Nikolai and Fianna, anxious to get started, make short work of their morning meal.

Brahmal enters their meal tent, closes the entry flap, then stands between them with a hand on each child's shoulder, "Now to our training camp," Brahmal vanishes with them reappearing in the blink of an eye. Only this time, instead of a desert forest they find themselves in a rain forest. The sound of tropical birds flying high above trickle down through the thick air.

"Where are we?" Fianna rubs sweat off her arm, "It's so sticky here!"

"We are near the entrance to the portal of my brethren. The portal of the Erthen. Here I will show how to open and enter a portal. You cannot not enter this portal, but your keys will work the same as mine though my key differs," he holds up his hand and the shape of an inverted triangle with a line through the middle of it appears, "This is my key. Follow me."

Five paces to their right, he sweeps aside a curtain of vines to reveal a small hidden chamber leading to several others. He motions for them to enter and follows them in.

"Here is where you will train until the moon reaches its apex in the night sky.

Fianna and Nikolai look at one another feeling the "shocking moments" pile high with every step they take.

"Are you afraid?" Nikolai asks her.

"No. But I think it's cuz I've gone numb. Mind, body, and soul...all numb."

Nikolai nods his head in agreement, "Me too. But we're here together, and as long as we train together, we are still on the same side. That much we can do, right?"

"Right. Same side...teammates, for as long as possible."

"Okay then. Deep breath and exhale. It's time to wake up. Mind, body, and soul..."

Fianna smiles, "Through winding paths we've come..."

"Taking Fortune's hand, fear we've none," Nikolai voices her thought as if it were his own.

Fianna can't help but laugh aloud, "Poets we shall never be."

TRAINING DAY

"First, we address the portal opening." Brahmal walks to a far wall covered in several metallic shapes. In the middle of the wall, he finds a circle with a symbol in its center matching the one on his hand. He places his hand over it and the wall appears fluid then translucent. Two tall immortal guards stand on the other side of the portal. Brahmal steps through the portal turning to face Nikolai and Fianna, "It's that easy," he steps back through the portal placing his hand over the symbol again and the portal closes.

"So, I'll be looking for a symbol shaped like my key," Nikolai intuitively holds his key up noticing its odd shape.

"Exactly. Moving on now. Keep up," Brahmal walks quickly to an adjacent room with a long table and chairs, "Sit."

Nikolai and Fianna instinctively sit on opposite sides of the table facing each other as opponents.

"Next lesson. How to nourish yourself on your journey —," Fianna interrupts, "Oh no worries there. We have credit cards!"

Brahmal sighs, "And did you see any fast food services near our current location?"

"Oh, right. I guess not."

"Besides, you are immortals. You will create your own sustenance—whatever your preference—yourselves."

Nikolai and Fianna ask, "How?"

"Close your eyes, imagine what it is you desire for food."

Nikolai and Fianna eagerly comply. A plate of Niamh's cookies and a mug of her iced tea appear before each of them. They burst out laughing seeing each other's wishful thinking sitting before them.

"Moving on," Brahmal heads towards another chamber. They grab a handful of cookies stuffing their faces and slurping the cold tea as they follow Brahmal through a maze of tunnels.

Brahmal leads them through two chambers stopping in a third. This chamber is filled with large boulders and tall underground canyon walls with a narrow river cutting between them. The chamber was portioned off with sections to mimic every climate on earth.

"This chamber will test the limits of your strengths and you will remember those limits,"

"Okay. Where do we start?" Nikolai is determined to master any short comings that may surface.

"Each of you have demonstrated great strength, speed, and tolerances beyond the normal human's skill set. But today you will compete only against each other."

"This should be interesting," Fianna remembers Nikolai having the upper hand in basketball from having memorized her moves long before they ever played. Now he would be competing with none of that advantage.

Over the course of the day, their only true physical weakness became quite clear—temperature. Whether it was mountain climbing, throwing house sized boulders, running or swimming they were equally skilled.

"Brahmal, may I ask a question?" Nikolai having finished a two hundred mile run in scorching sands leans on his knees gasping between gulps of air.

"Of course."

"If we are immortals why does the dry heat affect me so negatively and the wet heat affects Fianna negatively?"

"Even immortals are given challenges to overcome. Fate chooses those challenges. It is not for you to ask why, but for you to overcome and conquer them."

Fianna has finished swimming across the frigid river finally. She collapses on the riverbank shivering. Nikolai sits down next to her folding her in his arms, "Here let me warm you." They lie their heads on each other's shoulder. The frigid cold from Fianna meeting scorching temps from Nikolai converge violently to produce streams of twisting steam hissing in protest as it rises.

"Ha, ha, I'm sure there's got to be a funny side to this," Fianna laughs through chattering teeth.

Brahmal's eyes cloud over as he mentally checks the moons position. His eyes clear and he calls to them, "Moving on now!"

"God help us," Fianna uses a term she heard an opposing basketball coach mutter one day, "Wait a minute—we're gods," Fianna laughs as Nikolai helps her to her feet.

They jog to catch up to Brahmal who is already several paces ahead. Slowing their pace, they fall in behind wondering what is next.

"Technically, you are immortals borne of gods."

"Not yet gods?" Fianna feigns disappointment.

"Not yet." *Though I feel that will change soon.*

Through a maze of tunnels, they find themselves in a chamber looking more like an obstacle course.

"What is all this?" An exhausted Nikolai is nearly afraid to ask.

"This is where you will learn to change your present form into pure energy so that you might travel more efficiently. In your present form it would take you days to traverse from one side of the planet to the next. In your energy form you will travel the same distance in seconds."

"We can do that on our own?" Fianna's face beams with the possibilities.

"When did that happen?" Nikolai's frustration with being kept in the dark grows apparent.

"These powers were only released yesterday. You are old enough to make the wise choices to keep your powers hidden—and you *will* keep them hidden from all humans."

"Ah, I understand. You waited until we were old enough to control selfish impulses."

"I guess flaunt what ya got definitely don't apply here."

Brahmal eyes Fianna, "It appears you understand. Moving on now. I want both of you to close your eyes, relax, and imagine you are standing on top of that waterfall in the middle of the chamber."

Seconds later they are both ankle-deep in water, "Ew, I've got squishy socks now!" Fianna complains loudly.

"Meh, it's not so bad," Nikolai stands in the water too, but he's wearing water shoes.

"Hey, where'd those come from?"

"When I imagined myself up here it was with water shoes."

"Fianna imagines her own pair on, "Much better."

They spend the rest of their day vanishing and reappearing in different places, circumstances, extreme temperatures, and playing the occasional prank on one another. Fianna goes a bit too far imagining Nikolai as an overly large rat thus procuring her teacher's wrath. Brahmal turns her into a large ice cube—all but her head. He proceeds to lecture her with an extensive reading of the Divine Laws of Conduct between immortals which dare not be broken.

During all this Nikolai imagines himself a small feast of cookies and tea. He leans on Fianna's cube of ice savoring each bite of cookie mere inches away from her mouth.

"Go away, Nikolai or I'll be cramming those down your gullet once I thaw out," she whispers through smiling teeth while Brahmal's lecture drones on.

Nikolai smiles as two piping mugs of hot chocolate appear in his hands, "Tsk, I guess I'll have to drink both myself," he sets one atop the ice cube in front of her nose while guzzling the other, "Ah, feeling toasty."

The cube vanishes. She catches the mug, "Feeling vengeful!"

INTROS & MORE

"Cheers!" Fianna prepares to dump the mug over Nikolai's head, but Brahmal's patience is thinning.

"Stop! Enough of this childish behavior!" Brahmal bellows shaking the chamber. The mug disappears and the two of them look only slightly admonished.

"Sorry," a unified apology muffles a few smirks and giggles.

"Destiny arrives any moment. You will be on your best behavior if you know what's good for you."

His warning still hangs in the air when a breeze rustles through the chamber bringing the Divine with it.

"Good evening children of the Fyre and Merbatho," Destiny's greeting arrives on the breeze before her unusual blue eyes materialize followed by her pearly white form. Standing tall and regal she wears her dark hair floor length.

"You will kneel in the presence of the Divine," Brahmal scowls at the children kneeling himself.

Fianna kneels in awe of the statuesque goddess before her, "We did not know."

"We mean no disrespect," Nikolai's sincerity is felt.

"I know, and it is not your fault. You've been away too long from your home. No one to teach you the Divine Laws much less any of the social graces. Rise now. There is someone I want you to meet."

The three Majix appear. Nikolai and Fianna shout, "Ms. O'Shea!"

"I knew it, I told you she was connected," Nikolai reminds Fianna, "It's a relief to see a familiar face."

"You knew her as Ms. O'Shea, but her name is actually Niamh. This is her mother, Rionach and her daughter Maebh," Destiny introduces the Majix, "They will be helping you along your journey from time to time."

Destiny turns to Brahmal, "You may return home now. You've earned a rest."

Free of any further training involving the two charges brings a great relief to the burly Erthen. "At your will," a small sigh escapes Brahmal as he vanishes.
Babysitting...not my strong suit.

"Niamh, take Nikolai to the chamber of fountains. Let him swim awhile then tell him the story of the demigod repentant in love's wake."

Swim? Yes, yes, yes...I need to recharge. Nikolai's selective hearing never registers the mention of a story. He's at her side in a flash following her out of the chamber.

"Maebh, take Fianna. Let her bathe in the sunroom until her energy returns. Then you must tell her of the mother who mourns."

Fianna appears puzzled at first. *The 'mother who mourns'? Sounds depressing.* But the thought of soaking up some sun rays has her following Maebh in lost-puppy fashion.

"Little Mischief, show yourself," Destiny commands.

"Guess where I am," Fortune teases.

Destiny casually walks over to seat herself in a small chair and sets her feet upon its foot stool.

"Rude!" The stool totters angrily to the side transforming into the fuming goddess, "You are absolutely no fun at all," She plops down on a nearby chair grumbling, "Is my part in this tedious game finished yet?"

"You will have to ask Fate."

"Never mind," she already knows the answer.

"I personally would prefer you watch over the children. Their inherent immortal differences seem to be rising to the surface."

"And what should I do about it? It was not I who set the challenges between the immortals. Let Fate babysit them."

"Really? Shall I tell her, or will you be setting her straight on the matter?"

Fortune briefly contemplates her choices and their ultimate consequences, "*Fine*, I will resume my nanny duties. But don't be surprised if boredom clouds my judgment. I was rather entertained by the ice cube theatrics."

"Yes. We noticed."

Fortune is quiet a moment, "Who will tell them of the Portal of Allies?"

"Rionach."

"Speaking of— where has she gone?"

"I've sent her to the Emerald Isle until she is needed. Even one of the Majix requires recharging from time to time."

Fortune smiles mischievously, "Exactly...as do the Divine."

Destiny rolls her eyes, "When the games ends you may flit off anywhere you like."

"Promise?"

"I promise. Until then, keep a close watch on them. I've seen dangerous paths forming in the future. Paths of pride, greed, and resentment. Still, there are others full of empathy. Some intend to interfere with the game."

"When did this start?"

"Soon after Idalia had a change of heart."

"Then they are from the Fyre?" Fortune hisses.

"Actually, no."

"Then who?"

"The *Elementals*," Destiny's eyes burn angrily.

"But why?"

"Some side with the Fyre. They resent being summoned for frivolous means. Others side with the Merbatho. Some for the greed of offerings, some out of pride for their status among practitioners, and others are simply full of empathy for the human race."

"Hmph, I suppose after this game we will be extending a few Divine Laws to include the *Elementals*."

"Indeed. Until then I will fight their mischief—with Mischief," Destiny smiles at the twinkle in Fortune's eye, "They need you sister. Keep a careful watch."

"Not to worry, sister. It will be my pleasure. Why, I don't believe I remember ever toying with elementals. This should be fun," Fortune smiles and waves goodbye, "Toodles."

Destiny pours herself a cup of lavender tea and listens to the Majix as they reveal truths long hidden from the children. She listens to the internal battle within the children as they sit stunned into silence until finally each child knows and feels their individual immortal heritage.

Maebh and Niamh give an acknowledging bow of the head as they pass under a nearby archway leading their somber charges to their sleeping chambers. Destiny senses Fortune's energy following them.

Niamh stops at the end of a short hallway, "Here we are. Nikolai your room is to the left and Fianna your room is at the end of the hall. Since you have mastered your powers of visualization, I trust you can manage your own meals."

"Yes ma'am," Nikolai responds only half hearing as he stumbles into his room still overwhelmed with new revelations of the people who have been raising him.

"Thank you, I can find my way from here," Fianna treks the last dozen paces to her own room putting all her focus into each step. Her intellect and emotions a jumbled mess.

Nikolai finds a hammock hanging above a small pond of still blue waters. A simple visual of himself lying in it is all that is needed. Lying above the pond with his eyes closed he feels a cool breeze over the water soothing his frayed nerves.

Sleep, I need sleep then tomorrow—tomorrow? What new mind- blowing story-of-my-life comes tomorrow? Does it even matter? I survived this day. Tomorrow is another day and I swear I will do more than survive. I will conquer it!

Nikolai lets the sway of the hammock lull his mind into sleep's deepest ocean where worry and strife cannot swim.

Fianna enters her room to find it decorated in her favorite sunset hues. Her hammock swings between two ash trees with a small potted saguaro in the corner of her room. She kicks off her shoes and falls into the hammock relaxing into its gentle swing. A warm breeze softly kisses her face reminding her of so many carefree times lounging around her own backyard.

My entire world has changed since I last closed my eyes—literally! I wonder. Will tomorrow bring the straw that breaks the camel's back? No. I will not fold under pressure! With every fiber of my being, I refuse. So—bring it on.

Fianna's determined eyes finally close as she slips into a deep sleep with the swaying of her hammock.

Fate watches from the Seventh Plane, "They do not yet have the full physical strength of an adult immortal. However, their inner strength rival's any of their brethren."

Destiny returns to her side, "They will sleep while Fortune fortifies their resolve."

"I'm glad to hear she will continue looking after them."

"She protests—"

"Out of habit."

"Yes, but I think she's grown fond of them."

"Then woe to those who would oppose them."

ELEMENTAL QUIBBLE

Surean walks with her favorite undine through the Fyre Citadel corridors as a Fyre guard escorts them to Narceous' gardens. He leads them through a new maze of corridors as Narceous has been relocating her gardens to accommodate her newest additions. Reaching the end of a long corridor they pass through an archway of thick thorny vines filled with colorful birds loudly announcing the arrival of a Merbatho.

"Surean! I'm so happy you could make it. Come see my newest creation," Narceous greets her most unlikely friend with a hug.

"I wouldn't miss it," Surean's sincerity calms the chattering birds.

"I've been working on something especially for Fianna's return," Narceous' motherly enthusiasm is catching and Surean can't help but feel her own optimism creeping up.

Narceous opens a nearby door to an adjacent chamber. Searing heat rolls out, "Dubheasa, you may wait out here. I know the dry heat can be uncomfortable for undines," Narceous motions to a comfortable chair.

The beautiful dark-haired undine bows her head, "Thank you, you are most considerate."

Surean leaves with Narceous as the Djinn Earhard—who is never far from Narceous—arrives to take the place of the guard.

Earhard gives a respectful nod to Dubheasa before assuming his guard position with a purposeful regal stance.

"Greetings Earhard. You are looking quite well."

"Thank you, and you are gracious as ever," Earhard's eyes hold the faintest hint of affection.

"Will you be returning to the Fourth Dimension soon?"

"Not until the *Contest for Conquest* has ended."

"Me as well. Not that I am complaining. Surean's company is always delightful."

"Dubheasa, I do not believe I have ever heard you complain. You are probably the most agreeable elemental I have ever known."

She laughs and the two elementals continue exchanging pleasantries while they wait on their perspective goddesses to return. Finally, the two goddesses' voices can be heard nearing the other side of the door, "It's perfect Narceous. I'm sure she's going to love it."

"I can hardly wait for her return. Win or lose this foolish game—I simply do not care. You know, many Fyre thought the matter a waste of attention when there are so many other galaxies with much more pressing issues."

"You surprise me. The Merbatho thought the matter was a unanimous consensus amongst the Fyre."

"No, it was not. In fact, several later confided Gyntargh had been calling in favors amongst our brethren. If he had not been exiled by The Divine, Neilina would have done it herself once all was revealed."

Earhard's head, turned slightly toward the door, scowls with disapproval.

"Something said displeases you?" Dubheasa asks.

"Yes."

"You think mortals should lose access to elementals?" Now Dubheasa is scowling.

"Yes."

"But why? They are so fragile, and many are helpless."

"Many are strong and greedy. They command elementals of fire to do their bidding for frivolous tasks."

"Like what?"

"Fancy cars, jewelry, more money than they know how to waste. It is...demeaning. They have no true gratitude."

"Then simply demand an equal offering."

"That is not the point."

"Then what is?"

Earhard groans with frustration, "We should not be treated as one of their dogs sent to fetch a pair of slippers. Our station is worthy of respect."

"Agreed. But that is a matter of educating the practitioners."

Earhard looks hard at his beautiful friend. He sees nothing but selfless kindness and cannot help but temporarily concede the argument.

"Can we simply agree to disagree for now?"

"Of course, as you wish."

"Do you ever stop to think of yourself?"

"Naturally. And I am most happy when I am helping others find their happiness."

"If only humans were as altruistic as you."

"Actually, I am not altruistic at all."

"Explain."

"I receive great satisfaction in helping others accomplish their goals. Therefore, since I have received something in return, I am not being altruistic at all."

Earhard rolls his eyes, "I shall never win an argument with you, will I?"

"Most likely not. However, it is amusing when you try," Dubheasa teases Earhard as she would only do in their private conversations.

Narceous and Surean exit the new desert garden ending the elementals' friendly debate.

"The garden of rivers I have been preparing for Nikolai will also be finished soon. Perhaps you could bring some of the nopal tea you mentioned. We can share it on a beach."

"Do you think you will have at least one *warm* beach?"

"Yes, dear friend. Your comfort was a consideration in my design. When the children return, I expect to go on being your friend and you mine," Surean hugs Narceous before taking her leave.

"You read my mind," Narceous returns the embrace, "Let me know when your garden is ready for my visit."

Another guard appears to escort Surean and her undine back through the Fyre Citadel. Dubheasa and Earhard exchange formal parting looks as she leaves.

The goddess and her undine return to their own citadel in silence. Once they are back inside Surean's rooms she turns to Dubheasa, "Alright, out with it my child."

"I am sorry. I do not follow. Out with what?"

"I felt your hidden distraught the moment I left Narceous' garden. Did her Djinn upset you? Should I bring the matter to Narceous?"

Dubheasa's brow wrinkles slightly as she struggles with sharing a friend's opinion expressed in a private confidence, "It is nothing—I think. I do not want to betray the trust given in one's expressing an opinion."

"I see," Surean pauses to gauge the room's energy, "Yet, you are worried. Given the only topic of conversation was the children and game I am now worried too."

"Can you trust me to ensure the children will be safe and the game will remain fair?"

"This I would trust of you. But should variables of either change you will inform me."

"I promise. If it pleases you, I would leave now to make arrangements to ensure my word holds true."

"Do what you must, and if it needed, you may leave the Fifth Plane to keep your word."

"Thank you," Dubheasa takes her leave.

THE FOURTH DIMENSION

Deep within the vast space—where time sees all that is, was, and still yet may come—lies the origins of all elementals. It is where they gather to watch over other beings rendering aid when asked or—at times—commanded.

Once upon a time, humans relied heavily upon them for survival. Crops, weather, health, and protection were the order of the day. Then civilizations expanded and conquered the land, sea, and air. The humans' craving for power and greed became a constant whine in the winds.

Dubheasa enters through the Portal of Undines to the Fourth Dimension. Making her way past the throng of Sylphs, Gnomes, Djinn, and Undines like herself she finds her way to King Nixsa, the leader of Undines.

"Dubheasa!" The king greets her with open arms, "How wonderful to have you back," the slightest of scowls crosses his forehead, "All is still well between you and the Merbatho?"

"Oh yes, of course."

"Of course, it is. How could it be otherwise? You are the favorite of Surean!" Nixsa beams with pride.

"King Nixsa, I have returned early for your counsel. There is a matter I have promised to handle for Surean—regarding the children in the *Contest for Conquest* as well as the rules of the game."

"Then let us share our minds as one."

Nixsa and Dubheasa join minds while excluding all other elementals. Normally, their telepathic minds would resonate similar as humans in a crowded auditorium. A din overall but each able to focus on a single mind in order to communicate effectively. But occasionally, their minds all come together to listen to a communication from one or more of their kings where all are meant to hear. When privacy is desired the intent of exclusion is necessary.

Dubheasa shares her previous conversations with Earhard and Surean in great detail along with her own opinions.

"My dear child this would be a first," Nixsa worries, "Never before have elementals interfered in a game between the gods."

"Yes, I know. But I can feel *that* is about to change. I know and respect Earhard with all that I am. It grieves me to be in opposition to him. Believe me when I say, he has long been impatient with the mundane and menial ventures some of the immortals have imparted on him on behalf of the mortals. He is deeply offended, feeling no better than a human's dog fetching slippers for its master. The seed was already within him and Gyntargh of the Fyre did set it to bloom. He knows there is no law to stop our interference."

"Ah, I feel he has just arrived. If he has left the side of Narceous so soon after returning to the Fyre, I fear you are most correct in your assumptions. I will call upon him and the other kings now. We must come to a consensus on the matter before a decision can be put before all to hear."

"Thank you."

Nixsa closes his eyes reaching his mind out to the other elemental kings. A heated discussion puts the Sylphs and Gnomes siding with the Undines. Earhard does not yield.

"I move we bring the matter to our full domain and let open debate be heard before we make a final ruling," Earhard insists.

"Make the announcement," Nixsa saddened by a possible rift motions to the Herald of Elementals.

"Attention All!" The herald's telepathy interrupts all private conversations. The collective minds of the Fourth Dimension turn their attention to the kings and listen as one.

"A matter of debate has arisen for all to hear and consider. Each of your kings will present their argument and then all will vote on the matter. You will vote according to your own will and no one else. King Earhard will present his argument now."

"I have recently learned the Fyre did not wholly agree with Gyntargh's argument to reign in the human's misuse of elementals. For too long now we have endured their greed summoning us for the frivolous, petty, and power hungry. Now that the *Contest for Conquest* has begun, I say we support the female immortal called Fianna in her quest for her opponent's portal as there is no Divine Law prohibiting our help."

The salamanders—fire elementals—listen intently nodding their heads in agreement while several of the water, air, and earth elementals shake their heads in opposition.

King Nixsa rises to speak as King Earhard steps back, "While it is true there is no specific Divine Law prohibiting our interfering in the game there is still a matter of keeping the game fair. I do not believe for a moment Fate, Destiny, nor Fortune would be agreeable to our helping either immortal in finding their opponent's portal. I would advise caution to all," he yields to King Paralda.

"I agree with King Nixsa. This is new territory King Earhard proposes. Tread carefully. If you choose to help either of the children, it may be construed as cheating the game. However, that does not mean you cannot choose to help keep the game fair. May intuitive forethought guide you wisely."

King Ghobe of the Gnomes resonates genuine warmth and gratitude as he speaks next, "I think I speak for most or all of the earth elementals when I say—we have benefited as much as the humans from our current arrangement. Help is requested of us, offerings are provided to us, and in return we help the practitioner. A fair exchange is completed. I see no problem there. However, should the humans be required to ask directly of the immortals, and we are excluded...then exactly how do we benefit? This is an unknown. We may benefit little if any at all."

King Ghobe sits back upon his throne listening to the conflicting thoughts running rampant across the domain. The herald calls out to the collective din, "Quiet! You have heard all arguments to be presented. Make your decision and cast your vote now. Do we give permission for each elemental to act on their own will in the matter? Or, do we remain separate from the immortal's conflict?"

A large golden counter appears for all to "see" as the votes are given. The votes tally and Earhard smiles. Though he has narrowly won the argument he has not heard the private conversations already plotting against him. For the first time in all of their existence, the elementals meddle in the *Game of Conquest*.

From the Seventh Plane Fate and Destiny fume, but refrain from putting the elementals in check.

"As if the immortal children have not already been tested beyond your original plan," Destiny growls as fine threads form in the crystalline bowl circling Fianna's current path, "What tangled web they weave."

"They wish to play in the game, do they? Mischief, let there be Mayhem wherever elementals attempt to cheat the game."

A "My pleasure," echoes through the veil from the Fifth Plane.

While Fianna and Nikolai enter their final sleep phase —each still slumbers in a gently swaying hammock—a tiny faerie sits atop a waterfall in a nearby chamber. She holds a tiny silver mirror in one hand as she pats her new short golden curls, "Hmm, I do like this new look but alas, it simply won't do," Mischief sighs and disappears into a red puff of smoke. The smoke dissipates leaving a large red viper in its place.

"That'sss more like it. Time to hunt a few sssalamandersss."

The viper slithers high up into the craggy sides of the caves to hide above the entrance to Fianna and Nikolai's rooms. Her red scales changing color to blend with the cave wall. Black eyes narrow to thin slits as she awaits her first victim.

SALAMANDERS AFOOT

The immortal children awake with renewed energy and purpose meeting in the "hallway" of their sleeping chambers.

"Good morning, Nikolai," Fianna greets him with a familiar smile that would melt even the most indifferent heart. Nikolai's immortal heart sings with the sound of her voice.

She looks amazing considering the past few days.

"Good morning, Fianna. Did you sleep well?"

"Incredibly well, and you?"

"I feel like I've slept for days and could run a marathon."

"Race you back to the waterfall?"

"You're on!"

Nikolai sprints down the hall with Fianna racing by his side. They round a bend and then under the arch where they burst into the big cave laughing.

"Ah, that's more like it. I'm used to having my morning run although this morning's is a bit short. You know, I think I could run for days," Fianna sits on a boulder by the small pond collecting foam at the bottom of the waterfall.

"I know what you mean. As much as you need to run, I need to swim—and this tiny pond won't do."

"Hmm. I wonder," Fianna closes her eyes, faces the pond, and stretches out her arms. The pond instantly spreads out another few dozen feet.

"There that should do," she stands with her hands on her hips admiring her work.

Nikolai stands and closes his eyes. His clothes are instantly replaced with his favorite swimwear, "Join me? We appear to be the only ones milling about so early."

"A swim before breakfast and then we..." her smile fades.

"Race to find each other's portal. If I win humans retain their direct access to elemental help; you win they must grovel for it. And our human friends have no voice in the matter of debate," Nikolai finishes her thought with a sense of sadness.

"Maybe one day we will find ourselves on the same team—and fighting for our human friends," Fianna shrugs off her melancholy and swaps her clothes for swimwear, "Last one in serves breakfast in a rat suit!"

She springs for the water, but Nikolai dives and hits the water a split second before her. He surfaces with a cheesy grin.

"Why, I do believe you would look smashing with pink whiskers and a purple tail."

Fianna giggles and transforms herself, "As you wish." Fianna squeaks and dives below the waterfalls foam with a purple tail slapping the water before disappearing in the froth. She emerges again as herself. Wet red hair clings to her face framing a pair of mesmerizing green eyes momentarily stunning Nikolai. A sudden tidal wave crashing over his head puts his mind straight and present once again.

"Oh, someone wants to play dirty," Nikolai plops a cloud of foam over her head giving Fianna fits of sputtering as she claws furiously at the foamy bubbles fighting to find her way out.

Their playful bantering and water warfare are watched with amusement from multiple planes. But on their own plane, within their own training grounds, a pair of salamanders creep along the cave's floor hugging a jagged wall.

"What is this?" The smaller salamander whispers.

"They have become friends," whispers the other, "Not the norm in a *Contest for Conquest*."

"We cannot reason with this girl. She obviously would not forsake her friend. I can feel the connection the two have made. It is quite strong."

"Perhaps the energy you feel is coming from the keys and not the immortals."

"If you are right, we can use the keys energy to our advantage. I will mimic the energy of the Fyre, and the boy's key and compass will follow me giving the girl time to reach the Merbatho Portal," the small one surprises himself with his own cleverness, "I am brilliant. Am I not? Yes, yes, I am."

Suddenly both salamanders are caught up in a noose of scales raising them off the floor of the cave with their bodies imprisoned. The two elementals unable to transform from the physical body to one of energy become petrified with fear. Coiling scales spin them around to face a pair of angry black eyes sitting above venomous fangs. A Macabre of Mischief hisses sending shivers down their yellow spotted backs.

"Sssooo, you would cheat the Merbatho immortals from a fair game. Tsk, tsk. Those of fire should not leap so quickly."

"We've broken no Divine laws," the larger one quivers in protest, "No law bans elementals from the games."

"Divine Law states that no *BEING* may present an intentional unfair advantage for any particular contestant."

"We were only trying to serve the Fyre Citadel as is our calling," the small less than brilliant salamander cries out.

"Ssserve? Ha!" Mischief transforms into an angry breathtaking golden goddess.

"Now you will serve the humans for a thousand of earth's years. I hereby condemn you to serve as genies for your crime. How dare you interfere with a game between *gods*!"

"No, you can't do this!" the small once screeches.

"You dare to command the Mistress of Mischief!" She picks up a brass incense burner in one hand, transforms the salamanders to smoke and stuffs them inside.

"Perhaps this will teach you to test The Divine," Mischief seethes at the two trapped elementals with her eyes piercing through the brass wall sending them scurrying to the far corner of their new home, "Enjoy your new quarters."

She tosses the brass piece high in the air where it disappears landing somewhere in the middle of the Pacific Ocean.

Across the room the playful banter has long halted. Fianna and Nikolai quietly observe the scene. Already in their travel clothes, each looks at their own compass before exchanging a long hug and then quietly disappear.

Rionach, Niamh, and Maebh appear to stand before Mischief.

"We stand ready to serve The Divine," they declare in unison.

Niamh is to watch over Fianna, Maebh watch over Nikolai, and Rionach—once they've reached their perspective Watchtowers —you will inform them of the Portal of Allies and their options."

"As you will it, it shall be done."

I will be watching over all of you, but if you encounter any more elementals bind and hold them in their physical forms until I arrive.

***

On the Seventh Plane Narceous holds a crystal ball before King Earhard's face. She raises one eyebrow awaiting explanation.

"They were sent to assist your daughter in her quest."

"No, they were sent to appease your sense of ego," Narceous sets the crystal ball back upon its velvet post, "you should have consulted me first."

"Perhaps. But I did not mean for my soldiers to lure the boy away. My intention was for them to provide advice on the meaning of signs, vortexes, and ley lines. The same help that could be received from a human."

Narceous stares hard at Earhard feeling his energies for any signs of deceit. Finding none she errs to forgiveness, "In the future you will consult with me if and when you should decide to test unchartered waters. Understood?"

"Yes. As you will it, I will obey."

"Oh, Earhard. Even I need a break from all the formalities. Relax. I will not be removing your head today."

Earhard lets a smile of relief flash briefly across his handsome face, "And I appreciate it. May I return to the Fourth so that I may set limitations for my soldiers?"

"You may, but if any more elementals are lost for your ego—I will personally put you in a genie's lamp myself."

VORTEX HOPPING

Fianna stands atop Mt. Shasta, her fifth vortex, looking out over the blue expanse in forty-degree temps with a slight breeze and snow beneath her feet. Shivering slightly, she imagines herself beneath the Arizona sun to bring in its summer warmth to fill her.

"That's better," she lifts her compass in one hand and her key in the other wishing for the Merbatho Portal. The compass needle simply vibrates in place, "Well, I suppose that would have been too easy."

Walking along a precarious ridge she tries to instinctively feel for any vortex energies. She wanders with both key and compass in one hand waiting for any sort of sign. After a few hours of ambling about the mountain top with snow crunching beneath her feet she plops cross-legged to hover inches above the frozen ground.

"Seriously, the portal could be anywhere on earth, "she imagines herself speaking with the Divine Fortune, "I feel like I'm looking for a needle in a haystack—one humongous haystack!"

Placing her face in her hands she takes in several deep breaths to calm the rising tide of frustrations, "All I'm say'n is...a little help would be greatly appreciated. A sign...a teeny tiny sign is all I'm askin' for here."

High above her head Niamh watches from a large puffy cloud as a graceful translucent Sylph appears before Fianna. She senses no ill will from the Sylph, but rather a deep caring respect. The Sylph glides closer towards her speaking softly.

"Sweet child, you have been given all the signs you need. Seek that which you already possess." Fianna mistakenly takes hold of her key and compass. "No, my dear. Not those. It is not yet their time to aid you. They are not the only gifts you behold. Try to remember." The Sylph floats up into the blue sky passing across the sun's rays where she disappears into the light.

"Wait! Gifts, what gifts?" Fianna shouts with all her being, but the Sylph has gone, and she's left alone again.

"Awesome, *another* riddle to solve," Fianna grumbles aloud. For lack of an immediate solution, she produces her favorite breakfast bar with chocolate chips to chew on as she mulls over the Sylph's words.

"Not the only gifts I behold. Gifts? The gift to transform into energy and back to my physical body. Gifts of endurance, strength—a good sense of humor," she jokes to brighten her dark mood, "Yep, a lot of good they're doing me right now."

She holds up the last bite of her breakfast bar thinking of Nikolai. It was the last time she'd enjoyed one. Thinking of her BFF brings the memories of their many days spent researching the vortexes, ley lines, geology, and megaliths she suddenly jumps to her feet shouting out, "That's it!"

Fianna stretches her arms out and extends her hands palms up. She imagines the gift and it appears instantaneously

"Alright then. Now we're talking," she holds a stack of four books. Four books gifted to her and Nikolai by Niamh the night they set things in motion for their research trip. Suddenly two of the books disappear. She stretches out her hands, imagines them back and they reappear. Only this time a note written in Nikolai's handwriting appears with them.

You cannot keep all of them at the same time.

Fianna laughs out loud. Deciding she'll start with the first two books she returns to Nikolai the third and fourth books. A note appears in her open palms where the books previously perched.

Loser wears the rat suit at their first feast on the Fifth Plane!

"Funny boy, it's on now." Her musical laugh echoes passing through her open palms back to Nikolai.

"At least she's keeping her sense of humor," Nikolai muses aloud. A nearby roadrunner perched in a bush cackles as if answering him. He sips on a lemonade leaning back in his chair hidden far from the main trail and its hikers. Contemplating in a large open cave, having already investigated five vortexes himself, he takes advantage of the twenty-degree temperature difference from a blazing sun-drenched terrain outside the cave.

"Before I dive into these," he places the two books on a shelf floating mid-air to his left, "I think this deserves a bit more attention."

Nikolai retrieves a folded piece of parchment paper from his pocket. Carefully, he unfolds the paper revealing Fianna and his combined maps of vortexes, ley lines, and megaliths. He scrutinizes the drawing making note of several changes someone has made to the map.

"This map has been altered. The question is...when? Let me think now. The last time I really looked at it was prior to our starting our trip. I suppose Fianna could have made alterations to throw me off the trail...no. Not her style. If she can't win fair and square, she'd rather not win at all. THAT'S her style."

He grabs a plate of fruit and cheeses from the table on his right. Munching loudly on the grapes he wonders aloud with a full mouth, "If not Fianna who? And more importantly, why? Clearly tampering with the game is frowned upon by The Divine."

His nearby candlelight is snuffed out leaving him in near dark. Nikolai transforms to pure energy blending himself with the cave ceiling.

"Don't be afraid. I did not mean to steal your light," the candle flame returns to reveal Fortune with her golden hair trailing nearly to the floor of the cave.

"Oh, it's you," Nikolai transforms to stand before her.

"Yes, it is I."

"I am sorry, but I do not recall your name."

"Probably because you left before I could give it."

Nikolai blushes under her accusing stare, "Oh. We thought it time to begin the race lest anyone else overstep their place. We meant no disrespect."

"You are forgiven—this time," Fortune's smile almost reaches her eyes. Nikolai realizes she is not joking.

"How may I help you?"

"It is I who has come to help—rather inform—you."

"Oh?"

"You were wondering who altered your map. It was I. You had some miscalculations and terrible drawings that needed correcting. Unfortunately, I was called away before I could finish polishing it up."

"Is that why I ended up here?"

"Here? Oh, you mean in the middle of a hot dry desert void of anything near a vortex?"

"Yes. I do not understand. This area is supposed to be where those beings alien to earth traverse from this galaxy to another."

"You should stick to the books with the cypher. Humans often embellish tales. Besides, you are looking for a portal to another plane—another dimension—not a galaxy."

Nikolai face palms himself, "Ugh, what an idiot I am."

"You are many things, but an idiot is not one of them. Mistakes are too often made by both humans and immortals. You are no exception. Look to your drawings again and be on your way. I have corrected the most important ones," Fortune throws Nikolai a wink and disappears into the ether.

The cover of book four opens with the breeze of her departure with pages quickly following it until coming to an abrupt stop. Nikolai picks up the book. Metatron's symbol jumps from the page. The symbol hovers above the page a second before floating over to the corrected map to touch down on Fortune's drawing where it disappears.

SOLVING RIDDLES

Nikolai studies the drawing, "For some reason it reminds me of Fianna with its odd shape of a broken axe blade," He filters through his memories looking for where he first saw it. Then it comes to him, "No, no, no. It's freezing cold there—literally!"

A large shadow looms over the entrance to the cave out of nowhere, "What the—?" Nikolai cloaks himself as well as his little camp site he's set up.

As the shadow grows bigger, he prepares for an expedited transport to far-away places when the source of the shadow lumbers in wearing a bearded smile with rosy cheeks and a pint of ale in one hand, "That's right, my boy. Ya better be bundling up tight. There's a mighty hard wind blowin' across Antarctica, and Ross Island be no exception."

Nikolai lifts the cloak eager to meet the small Gnome, "Hello, who are you?"

"Ah, who am I—makes no matter. What matters is you be on your way and remember this—your little friend is no idiot either. There will be two coming into the homestretch for sure. You can count on it!"

"Antarctica is still a huge territory to cover. Any suggestions?"

The question no sooner crosses his lips and a bat flies out from the back of the cave chasing the gnome away.

"Thanks! Perfect timing," Nikolai shouts at the bat who does a deep dive towards him before transforming into the beautiful Maebh.

"Yes, it was. Another word out of that gnome and he'd be spending a millennial trapped in a bottle at the bottom of an ocean."

"I don't understand...again."

"The information elementals can share with you or Fianna is quite limited. They risk their own freedom with every word out of their mouth."

"Then why are they trying to help? Are elementals not very smart. I mean no disrespect. I only ask as I have no experience with them."

"Most often they are too smart for their own good. But in this game, there are many who do not want the humans' right to call directly upon the elementals to be withdrawn. Then there are the few who are tired of those humans who have abused the gift bestowed upon them by the gods themselves."

"Is this abuse of the gift common?

"Depends on who you ask. Opinions are divided."

"If there is no consensus on the matter, how can it be justified to punish all for the flaws of a few.

"Justice is rarely found where egos abound. You have traveled far and visited many places in the short time you left the caves. Sedona, Mexico, Giza, and this place—"

"Don't say it. Please, my own ego wishes to forget this blunder."

"Then be on your way now. The gnome was right. You are both nearing the homestretch.

Nikolai packs up his campsite with a wave of his hand, "Thank you, I will indeed be on my way now."

Nikolai leaves the beautiful Maebh with a wink of his own before transporting himself to Ross Island where he apparates to his human form bundled in a suit made for the frozen tundra of Antarctica.

However, in his rush to leave he did not notice the map of vortexes, and such had quietly vanished right before he broke camp.

Still back on the North American continent Fianna jumps from one vortex site to another till finally landing in the skies above the Bermuda Triangle.

From the eye of a hurricane below she watches the churning of the sea all around her. Waves as tall as mountains crash upon one another, "Yuck, saltwater is worse than frozen clumps of snow crunching under one's feet," she sighs accepting what she knows she must do, "No way out of it. You can do it," taking a deep breath—an old habit—she prepares to dive under those mountainous crashing waves when a salamander appears perching atop her red crown, "Wait! I have something for you. It's allowed—I checked and double checked!"

The salamander produces her and Nikolai's map which is now fully corrected.

"Huh, these aren't our drawings. And look! Someone has changed some of our calculations. That's some nerve," she grumbles as only a hot-tempered immortal could over a hurricane.

"Yes, but Lady Luck has shone on both of you. Find the drawing that speaks to you." The salamander looks up in the sky seeing not only Niamh but Mischief's angry eyes and he visibly cringes, "That is all I can tell you for now." The tiny elemental disappears into the ether.

Fianna sighs and transports herself to a small cafe on a tropical island to reconsider her strategy.

"I've been vortex hopping and searching ley lines to the point of mental exhaustion. If it weren't for sheer pride, I'd give Nikolai the win and wear the rat suit with a smile," she mutters to herself too low for any human to hear.

But Fortune posing as a blue parrot in a nearby tree catches every word. *Sisters, I think both children could do with a time out.*

Fate and Destiny agree, *Make it so.*

"Where would gods keep a portal? Surely not the every-day mundane place," Fianna rambles on turning the map several directions to study it until finally, "Hold the phones. What's this?" She squints and leans closer inspecting one of the drawings as she snaps her fingers to produce one of the two books she was studying earlier. She places the cypher edge on the map next to the books cypher, "Bingo! THAT has got to be the place!!"

Sitting in the western quadrant of the cypher lies a small picture resembling a broken boot discarded in several pieces.

"Now where have I seen this before? We were studying in Books and Brew—-but what were we studying?" She pauses in thought, "I remember, it was Pounamu—in New Zealand! Merbatho boy couldn't keep his eyes off it and now I know why."

Fianna guzzles the rest of her cantaloupe drink on her way to a large mound of giant elephant ears grouped together. She pretends to admire the huge leaves walking around it. Reaching the backside of the plants she transforms herself to energy visualizing the tiny island of New Zealand. But she is unwittingly intercepted.

"What is this? Perfect, more frozen snow making that wretched sound with my every step," Fianna replaces sandals with snow boots before trekking ahead full speed right into Rionach.

"Careful child. You must keep your head about you—always."

"Sorry Rionach, didn't see *or hear* you coming."

"I certainly heard you coming. Explain why you trek across the frozen snow making a sound you hate."

"I am not where I intended to be. I'm afraid my powers are running out."

"Your powers are fine. I've brought you to the North Pole as it is neutral ground for both of you. A temporary intermission has been called for both you and Nikolai to rest and regain your strength. Both physically and mentally. Transporting frequently at such a young age is abnormal for immortal children. We do not want you overtired."

An electric zap fluffs Fianna's hair with the arrival of Nikolai.

A perplexed look of surprise and slight irritation colors his face.

"Wow, I totally missed my mark this time."

"Forgive me, but I intercepted your travel plans. As I was explaining to Fianna, it has been decided to call a short intermission in the game for the two of you to rest. Young immortals are not usually allowed to transport so often much less on the Third Plane."

"Oh?" Nikolai's eyebrow questions Rionach.

"Yes, it is true. And never question one of the Majix. It is not your place."

"Yes Ma'am."

"I admit, I could do with a bed to stretch out on," Fianna breaks the tension in the air.

"Come with me. I will give you the rest you seek."
And more.

Rionach transports the three of them to a warm lodge. It's a quaint and simple place. A crackling fire fills the small room with a soft glow. Two large beds hug the same wall. Each suited for its intended occupant.

"Oh my, a bed never looked so good," Fianna kicks off her snow boots and throws herself on the bed. She stretches out glad for firm support beneath her body. A typical Fyre she is and will always prefer sleeping on a granite hard surface.

Nikolai lets go of an unexpected yawn, "Sorry, it seems exhaustion has finally caught up to me." He follows suit losing the snow boots and throwing himself on top of the covers of the waterbed. "Awe," a sigh escapes as tiny waves roll beneath him.

Rionach spells them into a regenerating sleep before either can utter another word. Deep within their subconscious she introduces them to the Portal of Allies.

GAME ON

Fianna and Nikolai awake together three days later to find Rionach has gone, but Niamh and Maebh remain watching over them.

"Good evening children," Niamh greets them.

"Good," Fianna's yawn pauses her greeting.

"Evening," Nikolai finishes her thought.

"Please come and feast before the game resumes," Maebh ushers them both to a table overfilled with food and drink.

"And when will the game be resuming—if I may ask," Nikolai inquires as he offers a plate of roasted chicken to Fianna.

Fianna in turn offers him a large plate filled with every known cheese on the planet, "Yes, I'd like to know as well."

"The game resumes in five hours," Maebh pulls out a chair for her mother before seating herself.

"You're both looking well rested," Niamh observes as she sits and pours herself a glass of red wine.

"I feel like a million bucks," Fianna exclaims with a chicken leg in one hand and spoonful of potatoes in the other.

"Sweet, you'll be in a great mood when you put those whiskers back on."

"Ha, ha. Your—so—funny," Fianna counters lamely in between bites of chicken and potato, "I can't believe how hungry I am."

"Right?" Nikolai is puzzled himself as he empties a quart of milk in one shot.

"Well, you have been asleep for three days," Maebh states nonchalantly.

"*Three Days!*" Fianna and Nikolai shout in unison with a spoon still held high as her nose and Nikolai sputtering milk everywhere.

Maebh smirks satisfactorily having received the appropriate shock, "Why yes, three days. All your vortex hopping saps the energy right out of you."

"Okay, and what are we supposed to do till midnight after we've eaten?" Fianna suddenly feels restless.

"You are to remain here and then you may leave at your leisure,' Niamh finishes her wine and sets her glass down, "And now we will take our own leave."

"Until we meet again," Maebh leaves them with a wink before she dissipates into thin air.

Niamh's form dissipates but her voice lingers with a final bit of advice, "There are many choices along your paths. Your compass will show you the way if and when you listen to your heart's true desire."

Fianna looks at Nikolai to roll her eyes, "Don't know about you, but when we're done it will be too soon if I ever have to solve another riddle."

Nikolai's brow is furrowed as he contemplates the words, "True desire?"

"Your guess is as good as mine."

"I suppose."

"I propose we conserve our energy till midnight and amuse ourselves with a card game or two."

"Agreed."

Nikolai and Fianna pass the hours with poker—Nikolai usually winning due to his amazing poker face skills—

until some invisible clock begins an ominous clanging as it counts down to midnight.

"See you at the finish line," Fianna throws him a cheesy grin.

"I'll be there waiting on you," Nikolai laughs and hugs her.

The clock strikes its final chime, the fire blows out, and two immortals leave blue electric lines dancing in their wake. The small quaint lodge fades into the frozen ether of the North Pole.

Fianna lands with sandaled feet on a sandy beach of Spirits Bay at the tip of New Zealand's north island at the exact moment Nikolai plants his snow boots upon Ross Island's Erebus Ice Tongue.

A warm breeze carries a strange energy over Fianna's face. Tiny swirls of sand dance behind it as it travels up the beach towards a small peninsula.

Fianna looks at her compass. Its needle does nothing more than vibrate in place no matter which direction she turns.

"Still nothing from you, eh? Guess I'm left to follow whatever is heading down the beach." Fianna sighs and half skips to catch up to the swirling sand.

Nikolai, having found no help with his compass either, treks along an ice tongue contemplating which of two volcanoes is most likely to have a portal for the Fyre—Mt. Terror or Mt. Erebus.

"One of these is supposed to have an actual pool of lava at the bottom of its crater," He reaches for book four and thumbs through the pages, "These frigid temps have frozen my memory. Ah, here it is...Mt. Erebus." He looks up, up, and up until finally locating the top of the mountain in the moon light, "Yeah—not climbing that monster."

Nikolai hovers midair in the middle of the crater looking down at a pool of molten lava far below, "What now? Not seeing any doorknobs with a keyhole here."

As Nikolai considers his next move Fianna reaches the far side of the peninsula. She looks out over Spirits Bay, "Okay. End of the trail. Now what?"

Fianna sits cross legged on the ground and produces book two in her hand. Flipping through the pages, searching for any clues, she sees Metatron's cube mysteriously appear in the top corner of a page, "I'll take that as a sign."

Skimming over the page she finds a passage with an identical symbol matching another on her parchment map.

"Who'd have thought that one would be of any significance. I guess it makes sense though. Nikolai would have known." Fianna dons her swimwear in a melancholy mood, and proceeds to the dive point for a long underwater swim to the Merbatho Portal.

Back at Mt. Erebus Nikolai has perched himself below the rim of the crater with a heat shield protecting his fleshly body from the volcano's lava lake.

"Okay, Metatron. Show me the Fyre's portal," Nikolai calls out hoping for another sign. Instead, book two lands in his lap.

"Right, no freebies in this game," he picks up the book and flips through pages until noticing one with Metatron's cube in the lower corner, "What have we here now?" For the second time, Nikolai is grateful for Fortune correcting their parchment map. A passage he once thought inconsequential now aligned with their map makes perfect sense. He smiles wryly, "Fianna would enjoy my blundering over this one." With a sense of gloom and procrastination Nikolai hikes down the long trail to the lava lake—the Fyre Portal.

Myriads of immortals and elementals watch the *Contest for Conquest* from their perspective dimensions anxiously awaiting the impending *finale*. Though Nikolai and Fianna could quickly transport themselves to the portals they choose to prolong the race as if neither wants the win. This unusual delay causes a rippling stir across the Fourth and Fifth Planes.

"I wish one of them would open a portal and be done with it so they can come home," Narceous cries and Surean puts an arm around her as she dabs at her own tears.

"We have waited this long...they will be home soon," Surean tries to console her friend though she shares her apprehensive impatience.

Within the Fourth Dimension tensions run high. The fire elementals' emotions run the gamut from disappointment to outright anger while the majority of the other three elementals feel hopeful for an alliance between the children.

Saltwater washes over Fianna's toes startling her out of her own melancholy. The key of twelve senses the Merbatho Portal and calls to it. A rainbow of light bubbles to the surface several yards into the bay rolling its way to the shore. Fianna dives into the water following the colorful trail. Diving deeper and deeper until finally reaching a sea stack carved with a symbol matching the key around her neck that now pulls itself—and Fianna—towards the symbol.

Fianna swims with effort to hold herself away from the sea stack, "I know my brethren wish me to open the Merbatho Portal. But it is not my heart's true desire. With all that I am...I wish to be on the same side as Nikolai. We are brethren. We are unique equals."

With the words uttered the Portal of Allies connects to her compass spinning the needle to point the way.

Back in the crater of Mt. Erebus Nikolai has reached the lava lake. He stretches out his hands and it solidifies. An obelisk rises from the cooled lava bed with a carved symbol matching his own key of twelve. Like Fianna's, the key struggles to find its way home.

Nikolai catches the key before it reaches the portal, "No! I don't know why, but I can't. I want to go home, but not like this. When I leave this plane, I want to do it with Fianna's hand in mine. Even though we are unique individuals from different Citadels, I know combining our individual unique traits we are stronger together." Niamh's words rush back to him, 'There are many choices…', and though they are thousands of miles apart, both he and Fianna hear the echo of a dream.And when your heart's truest desire is unveiled

Compass and key will lead you to the Portal of Allies
Alas you must wait for your answer to be revealed
Before you may return home where the golden portal leads

The two immortal children close their eyes, holding compass and key while each is thinking of the other, they feel themselves transported in the blink of an eye to...

PORTAL OF ALLIES

The familiar smell of cookies and a special kind of tea fill the senses. Nikolai opens his eyes to stare unblinking in silence as he waits for Fianna who is actually standing less than a foot behind him.

"I thought you'd never get here," Fianna leaps to hug Nikolai from behind.

Nikolai turns and catches her up in his arms, "Fianna!" He holds her close a few more moments not fully convinced he isn't hallucinating, "I was there Fianna. I was right at the Fyre Portal and I could not do it. There is no victory if you're not at my side."

"I know, me too. I dove to the ocean floor to find the Merbatho Portal. But I couldn't go home without you coming with me—you and me on the same team. That's how it should be."

"Then I hereby offer an alliance. For today, tomorrow, and ever more."

"I hereby agree—whole heartedly—to your alliance."

"Wonderful," Nikolai starts to chuckle, "now how do we get home?"

Fianna grabs her compass and key, "My compass has gone quiet again."

"Mine too. By the way, it's nearly pitch dark in here. Where are we?"

"Lights!" Fianna commands and the room fills with floating candles, "Are you kidding me?"

"Books and Brew...the Portal of Allies?"

"Almost," a gruff voice from the past answers.

"Viktor?" Nikolai is surprised he is still on the Third Plane. A light switch flips on and the small bookstore is fully lit.

"Yes, Nikolai. We stayed to guard the portal."

"We? As in—" Fianna is interrupted by a familiar voice.

"As in we hoped you would return," Sahana's voice is as comforting as ever.

"I was allowed to know all that you are and stay with Viktor," Alicea's sweet voice follows and she emerges from behind Viktor.

Fianna and Nikolai rush to the first family they ever knew to embrace them. Alicea's tears stream silently down her face in relief.

"I can't tell you how relieved—and happy—to see the both of you again!"

"We were afraid you would never forgive us for our part in the game," Sahana's voice brims with emotion.

"I would understand if you did not forgive me," Viktor places his hands over Nikolai's shoulders.

"But I do forgive you," Nikolai's sincerity fills Viktor's heart, "It's time we all go home."

"Um, Nikolai? You and I still haven't worked out that riddle—remember?" Fianna whispers sarcastically.

A twinkle from the golden plate still hanging on the wall catches his eye, "Perhaps I have."

"Huh?"

Nikolai holds his key up facing the golden plate with the etched keys that match their own, "Let's go home."

Fianna holds her own key up to the golden plate. The etched shapes lift from the plate becoming one key.

Nikolai and Fianna's keys glide together becoming one then absorb the golden key. The tiny room fills with a rainbow of colors swirling into one beautiful arch. Beneath the arch stand Narceous and Surean.

"Children, welcome home," Narceous' embraces her daughter as Surean reaches for Nikolai.

"My child, you have been missed more than you will ever know," Narceous holds her daughter's face kissing her forehead.

From the Seventh Plane three Divine goddesses watch the reunion with relief.

Fate, happy they've returned home, considers the ease with which they conquered their challenges, "I must present these two with a next level challenge—after they've rested, of course."

Destiny is filled with hope, "Perhaps the Fyre and Merbatho Citadels may find a lengthier peace now."

Fortune finds elation knowing she is free to 'flit off anywhere' she likes now that the game has come to an end, "Let me see now. Where can an immortal find a bit of entertainment?" She waves her hand and a portal showing the entire Milky Way Galaxy spins round and round. She snaps her fingers and it stops instantly, "Ha, Earth again! Time to jet, dear sisters. But first a quick visit to the Fifth," Fortune disappears with her usual mischievous smile.

Back on the Third Plane, Viktor takes a deep steadying breath and enters the portal with Alicea fully expecting some form of formal punishment for his dastardly act.

Bowing before Surean he humbles himself publicly, "Goddess Surean, I await your judgment."

Surean's eyes blaze but only briefly, "Victor of the Fyre. You left this plane a despicable demigod with no redeemable qualities. And yet something—or someone—has completely refined you. You have taken great care of my grandson and we have seen the love you have for him and he has for you. Nikolai has forgiven you and so shall I too—though do not think it be easy."

"I humbly offer you my deepest and sincerest apology."

"The Merbatho accept your apology."

"If it pleases the Citadels, we would like to attend the children's first feast and then return to our home on the Third Plane."

"I am sure it is agreeable to all," Surean attempts a polite smile.

"Yes, yes. It is agreeable to all," Fortune's surly voice arrives before the Divine goddess arrives in her silver fairy form.

The Citadels bow in her presence despite her petite presence. Too many having experienced the wrong end of her powers first hand.

"Fortune, your presence at feast would be a blessing," Narceous bows as she extends the formal invite.

"I am sure I agree with you. However, Lady Luck has been sorely missed on the Third Plane, so I am afraid I have got to run. But first," she flits over to Nikolai and Fianna, "I do have a blessing to hand out. Children, you have shown an inner strength and tenacity in overcoming that which could have destroyed a lesser immortal child both emotionally and physically. Therefore, I wish to bestow a small gift upon you both."

"Thank you, that is—too kind of you," Nikolai nearly stutters remembering her wrath on the salamanders.

"Yes, too kind." Fianna knows not what else to say to one so powerful.

"It's but a small thing really, but I think it may serve you well in the future. Today, I bestow upon you both the blessing of great intuition, logical discernment, and the gift of unraveling any and all puzzles and/or riddles—as well as double talk, which humans are prone to use far too often."

"But—but we are home on the Fifth Plane now," Fianna stammers, "why would we need to decode anymore riddles much less double talk from humans?"

"Why indeed?" Fortune giggles and whispers, "Fate has you in her sights. I think she wants to see what you're really made of," her laughter echoes among the Citadels as she flits away from the Fifth Plane.

"Awesome," Fianna looks to Nikolai for additional thoughts.

"Feast today, Fret tomorrow?"

"Yuck, you have got to work on those witticisms of yours." Fianna follows Narceous and Surean as they turn for the Square of Commons where a great banquet has been set for their first feast.

"Oh come on, it wasn't that bad," Nikolai nudges her with an elbow.

"You're right. It wasn't bad. Horrid would be more accurate."

Narceous and Surean smile at each other loving the banter following behind them.

Far away Fate smiles too, "Feast today and tomorrow! You've certainly earned it. Rest well children. Quite soon you will hear it. You will hear the labyrinth that even now calls for you across the folds of time.

EPILOGUE

In the passages of time elementals do dwell
Call upon them if you will.
Do be forewarned, you should be greedy not
Lest their anger be too hot!

Though a celebration resonates through the Fifth Plane and humans retain their right to call on the elementals at will and without restriction there remains a goodly portion holding a grudge amongst the Fire elementals.

The Divine clarifying their limitations in any game between the gods only fuels a rebellion already simmering below the surface of polite conversation.

Fianna's name is all too often spoken with disrespect and animosity within a particular circle of the Djinn.

Fate has set new challenges for Fianna and Nikolai as Destiny observes changes in her crystalline bowl. Lady Luck will keep herself entertained on the Third Plane until her sisters call upon her once again.

Signs of a new game waft across air currents carried by the Sylphs, and humans go about their lives blissfully ignorant of all that lies beyond their tiny fishbowl lives.

www.ingramcontent.com/pod-product-compliance
Lightning Source LLC
Chambersburg PA
CBHW041138110526
44590CB00027B/4063